MGM MAKES
BOYS TOWN

MGM MAKES

BOYS TOWN

To David Potash,
    with all best wishes!
Welcome to Curry College !!

William Russo

WILLIAM RUSSO & JAN MERLIN

To order additional copies of this book, contact:
Xlibris Corporation
1-888-795-4274
www.Xlibris.com
Orders@Xlibris.com
33386

CONTENTS

1: FLANAGAN AND MAYER 7

2: MGM AND BOYS TOWN 20

3: THE STORY OF MANY SCRIPTS 30

4: TRACY and ROONEY... 41

5: ON LOCATION AT BOYS TOWN 55

6: BEHIND THE SCENES AT BOYS TOWN 67

7: THE BOYS AT METRO 85

8: SHOOTING THE PROLOGUE AT MGM 99

9: SHOOTING THE SECOND HALF AT MGM 115

10: POST-PRODUCTION 129

ACKNOWLEDGEMENTS 147

BIBLIOGRAPHY 149

*Louis B. Mayer and Father Edward J. Flanagan
meet at MGM in 1938.*

1

FLANAGAN AND MAYER

What extraordinary men they were!

Spencer Tracy thought so . . .

Louis B. Mayer and Father Edward J. Flanagan were alike in their Horatio Alger American success. Each man was born in Europe; L.B. always celebrated his birthday on the 4th of July, though his actual date was likely July 12th. Edward Flanagan was born on July 13th, the year after Mayer. Both had visions of their future. They immigrated to a world they firmly believed offered hope and a chance to lead a productive and creative life. Each man celebrated his new beginning in America with a life measured by generations to come.

The Home for Boys found its roots in 1917 near Omaha, Nebraska, and Metro a year later in California. By 1938 when a movie of Boys Town was filmed by MGM, the studio in Culver City and the home for boys were both about 160 acres. One was called the Dream Factory, and the other dubbed a Character Factory.

Both the priest and the producer believed in treating the denizens of his world like family. Each thought family values was the key to happiness. In the late years of the Great Depression, these two worlds came together: fact and fiction melded into a classic motion picture named *Boys Town*. Louis B. Mayer and Edward J. Flanagan made it all possible with a legendary collaboration.

Born in Roscommon County, Ireland, Edward Flanagan left his youthful home to start his adult life in a new land. His beginnings may be traced to a trip in the summer of 1904 to the United States upon a White Star liner. At this age, he knew his calling. Unable to matriculate, caused by health problems, at St. Joseph's Seminary in New York, he never gave up his idea to become a priest. Staying in Omaha during the summer of 1907, he made the acquaintanceship of an important member of the Catholic Church.

Enjoying the mentorship of the Archbishop of Omaha, Richard Scannell, he found himself in Rome in October of 1907. Again, respiratory illness forced him to withdraw. When a new term began at the University of Innsbruck, Austria, he went there to study theology. At last able to finish his studies, he was ordained a priest on July 26, 1912.

Back in Nebraska, Father Flanagan served in several small parishes around Omaha and O'Neill. He worked as Assistant Pastor in O'Neill and at St. Patrick's Church in Omaha. There, he learned the drought led to a rise in homeless adult wanderers "among the younger men, especially. There seemed to be little hope." Eager to help others by the winter of 1916, he began his Workingmen's Hotel to provide support for transients and vagrant men who were homeless or jobless. Fifty-seven men, some called hoboes, stopped by in first week of his hotel.

In his unpublished manuscript, *His Lamp of Fire*, Father Flanagan noted how "I used to wander about the streets, wondering how all this suffering could be." He believed his hotel for nomadic men could make a difference. The place was instantly overbooked. The priest offered a "young man" who was particularly forlorn a job as a desk clerk at night. In his manuscript he noted, " . . . We became fast friends . . . his accent was pleasing." The young man claimed to be a European count, which also intrigued and amused Flanagan.

He soon realized, "I was working with the wrong period of life." The older men were hardened and resistant to change. His efforts made him a target of the criminal element. He was warned that he made himself open to blackmail for his nocturnal visits to hotels to visit various pleas for help. In one instance, Father Flanagan concluded he was about to be "framed at an old, dilapidated rooming-house."

The priest worried in his memoir: "one's good intentions may also be misinterpreted." His mind was changed thoroughly and for all time by "a lad of about 14" who showed up on his doorstep in need of help, but gave the impression he was tough and independent. Father Flanagan said his name was "Bob Harper," but this was likely a pseudonym. It was this young man who turned Flanagan's mission away from older men and to teenagers and pre-adolescent. He discovered now he was "definitely interested in boyhood." He wrote of "a wonderful quality of youth that nothing ever seems impossible." In the Preface to his manuscript, he dedicated the work to homeless boys. It was his hope that those "who read this book will better understand the rugged, neglected boy."

At this point, Father Flanagan spent time visiting the juvenile courts. There he'd pick out certain boys he believed were suitable to his care, his philosophy, and his treatment. He put his focus on boys, aged 12 to 15, starting with five who became the foundation of his program. Following his plea and assurance, the five youngsters became his charges by the court's opinion. Two were brothers. Within a week he had fifteen wards. Borrowing $90, he rented a home at 25th and Dodge Streets and officially opened Father Flanagan's Boys' Home on December 12, 1917.

Money to care for the increased numbers meant that the priest had to find new ways to reach the generosity of the public. As February began, he printed the first issue of *Father Flanagan's Boys' Home Journal*. He was inventive, with an entrepreneur's spirit. Whatever it took to help the boys, he gave of himself. In spring of 1918, he needed a bigger place as the traffic of boys swelled. He sought a former German American meeting house, fallow now and untouched, owing to the war and its anti-German feelings. Flanagan shared none of that. To him the good fortune for his boys was that a house came to them when they needed it most. So on June 1, 1918, the boys moved to the abandoned German-American home on 13th Street.

Acquiring new space, he felt compelled to find a strategy to attract additional boys: Flanagan started a baseball team, which brought increasing numbers of ragamuffin youths to his Home. All boys involved in his program adhere to the "Honor System," a code on which their behavior, and their ties to each other were kept within the confines of the association with the Home. That was now the spot of their unquestioned loyalty. Father Flanagan put much faith in the loyalty boys gave him.

The program grew exponentially, and Father Flanagan believed he experienced a miracle, or at the least a sign that he was blessed and his venture foreordained. He rocked a pained little boy with an earache all night long. Without funds for medicine or other treatment, he could only give his personal comfort. In the morning the child had improved, and, as a consequence, he knew his life's calling.

Born in the Ukraine near Kiev, Louis B. Mayer's father and mother escaped to England, then to Canada. Their instincts saved them from anti-Semitic pogroms to descend in the years to come for Russian Jews. Once in Canada, Mayer's family stayed in Saint John, a small city with few Jews. It meant Louis learned how to assimilate at an early age. He had a knack for taking on whatever style, personality, and information needed to socialize with all kinds of people.

At the beginning of 1904, Louis moved from New Brunswick to New England; like so many at the time who found personal fates and fortunes were better served by leaving the Canadian Maritimes for the Hub of Boston, he abandoned Canada. He developed ecumenical skills, became mainstream and non-secular in style and demeanor. Having suffered a harsh life and a hard father, he also faced anti-Semitism. Louis Mayer's childhood epitomized the similar hardship that moved Father Flanagan a generation later to rescue boys from uncaring situations.

By 1908, Mayer opened the Orpheum, a movie theatre in Haverhill, Massachusetts, offering organ music and attractive surroundings. He loved those entrancing flickers, and made the burgeoning experience a pleasant one for women viewers, who usually shunned the nickelodeon. Soon, he branched out to legitimate theatre.

In 1912 he proudly became an American citizen and brought opera and stock company performing troupes to his Colonial Theatre in Haverhill. Actors like Maude Adams appeared on his legit stage and appreciated him, raving to New York actors about the stylish Boston impresario.

Expanding his vision, he built a stage theater in Lawrence, but realized he was bigger than New England. His desire to grow caused him to relocate next to New York and Pennsylvania.

Mayer formed American Feature Film Company, promising "wholesome films," the *imprimatur* for which he would become world famous. Making money from distributing *The Birth of a Nation*, he entered the social circles of Cecil B. De Mille and D.W. Griffith. He was a pioneer in the industry as much as they, and he would be the man to give the giant creative talents a platform to do their best work.

At the start of 1915, he bought out Metro Pictures in New York. Within three years he sold all his Boston/New England holdings—taking another leap into the notion of a Dream Factory. He moved to a little town called Hollywood, where climate might make filmmaking a year-round endeavor. Apart from orange groves, it was an unsettled locus. He could walk to work in the early days. Wandering the Hollywood streets, he saw other film companies at work in the back lots and studied their techniques. His absorbing of knowledge was a lifelong effort.

If he learned anything from these perambulations, it was: "I want high-class people" to be the rock of his new studio, and he endeavored to hire just that personality type. He loved movies from the start and described what he wanted to writers and directors. Though he never tried his hand at either creative profession, he had an unerring sense of his own insights.

When he produced Buster Keaton's *Go West,* the company added the name Mayer to the Metro-Goldwyn company name, and he was on his way. An uneducated man, he was sophisticated enough to know his limits and work to expand them. He'd ask someone to define words he heard in sentences and polished his syntax and mastered a plain mid-Western accent.

As the Hollywood scandals featuring Fatty Arbuckle and the Hearst troubles of the 1920s swirled around him, he kept his inner gyroscope on steady. He knew what was important and never lost track. Mistrustful of fame and the poison of bad publicity, he built his world, organized the studio, edited the stories, assessed the stars—but wisely left the nuts and bolts of motion pictures to men like Irving Thalberg, his creative foil at Metro-Goldwyn-Mayer. Since he wanted "classy films for the middle class," as biographer Scott Eyman astutely commented, Mayer gave Thalberg great latitude in the 1920s to produce his pictures, but it was Mayer who made discoveries like Greta Garbo and showed faith in people and projects.

As one might expect, Louis B. Mayer suffered many disparaging comments made about himself and his career. One critic commented the producer was a "rattlesnake." Others despised his power and arbitrary decisions. Many writers, in particular, disliked him, his style, his conservative Republican politics, and contributed to the notion that Mayer epitomized parvenu Hollywood. Though Mayer lacked the classical education training of Father Flanagan, their politics and patriotic fervor were a matched set.

Father Flanagan too had his early detractors. Not everyone supported his pioneering efforts in child treatment, and many thought he was misguided and permissive, allowing hooligan boys free reign. His opposition to punishment in any form also went in the face of prevailing attitudes of society.

When Father Flanagan began to chastise publicly political leaders, like the Governor of Washington, over the trial and sentencing of a twelve-year-old boy charged with murder, the priest interjected himself into secular life. He risked a backlash that society believed: priests ought to stick to Church matters. There was deep feeling that his incorrigibles were running amok. Segregationists were alarmed at his attitudes about racial harmony; he was criticized for letting white, Chinese, and Negro boys live together without any attempt to keep them separated. Some insisted his system lacked any real punitive sanctions.

Both Flanagan and Mayer were deep believers in family values and political conservatism, exemplified by support of men like Douglas MacArthur. Louis Mayer left in his will a stipend of ten million dollars to Cardinal Spellman of New York whose moral codes were among the most conservative of his times.

If, as Mickey Rooney stated, Mayer was running the General Motors of entertainment, then Father Flanagan was doing his best to create a publicity machine like the one Mayer ran so efficiently. In his own manuscript book, the cleric was coy about the identity of the man who gave the original cash to pay the rent on a house for the boys that the priest cared for. He knew that he could entice donations by hinting to some audiences that the donor was Jewish, or in other cases, a Mason. These played the ecumenical card that Flanagan saw as the foundation for his new home for boys.

In early 1917, the priest's boarding rooms were bursting with tenants. He had fifty boys needing and asking for his assistance. Taking a cue from Hollywood, Father Flanagan realized the benefits of publicity. He organized a rudimentary booster club for his activities, which he called the Omaha Mothers Guild. Creating another form of community outreach, he started a magazine to let the state's citizens know what he attempted to do for wayward boys. If he were not shameless about the image of the boys given to the public, he was at least shrewd. A crippled boy taken in was named Tommy. Unable to climb stairs, the child was given a "brother" of the home who'd carry him on his back.

The image of older boys carrying younger ones around the house was common, and the priest made sure the world saw its symbolic value. Three brothers, the Koch boys, arrived barefoot in July, aged 15, 13, and 9. These early brother teams inspired Father Flanagan to find a motto, "He ain't heavy; he's my brother . . . ." In his unpublished story, Father Flanagan cited a particular boy, unnamed, who was the epitome of the concept, his model for the idea. At the end of March in 1921, he sent his first solicitation letter to a wide audience, appealing for funds to support the Home to Catholic residents in eastern Nebraska and western Iowa.

Overseeing the spectacular growth of his enterprise, Father Flanagan found himself with a demand for public appearances. In the way that Mayer had his Thalberg, the creator of the Boys' Home relied on Father Harty to handle the daily duties of the home. He also enjoined two nuns to assist. By the 1920s, Father Flanagan's operation attracted such attention that courts were remanding custody of boys to him. Foot traffic also continued to swell the ranks with boys walking in off the streets. The priest met a throng of celebrities like Lou Gehrig, Tom Mix, Babe Ruth, Will Rogers, all the role models whom contemporary boys admired. The company he kept put him in the same league.

Long before the concept of dyslexia was discovered, Father Flanagan noted some problems with his boys and the traditional school system of Omaha. After taking the boys to school in a horse-drawn wagon, he found complaints from the boys and the school authorities about their learning abilities. Flanagan realized many boys had special needs not addressed with the Omaha Public School System. It was then he branched out into creating his own private school, giving attention to the needs of these special learners.

Louis Mayer had a like respect for the needs of his charges. They came to him with temperament and talent, not always an easy combination for the administrator and authority of their studio operation. Mayer declared: "I hire people for their brains and I'm not such a fool that I don't let them use them." He liked channels and bureaucratic structure; a chain of command gave him better use of his time. He was also opposed to silly superlatives about mediocrity. "Tell the truth, but make it attractive; sell your product, but don't oversell it."

According to Father Flanagan, there may not be any bad boys, but Mayer knew there were many misbehaving actors. As a remedy, he hired Chief Whitey Hendry to police his little community; Mayer's security force was like a babysitting clearinghouse and sanitation department combined. Mayer was also close to the local District Attorney, Buron Fitts; it gave the head of production a better means of keeping his entertainment product pleasant and image-conscious.

Mayer's publicity unit expected to control fan magazines by feeding them pictures and stories. One scriptwriter who was there observed, "Louis Mayer was a supreme organizer, very well setup to run a major studio operation. But in many ways he was overbearing, running things in a very high handed dictatorial way, and the studio was almost like a little fascist state." The biggest detractors to the system were writers who disagreed with Mayer politically and aesthetically.

Each major MGM star was assigned a publicist. In contemporary celebrity worlds, this staff member might be a part-time security force, bodyguard, and sometimes a lover, a procurer, or a spy, really reporting all information directly to the front office. It made for some a dependency. One star decried, "MGM created a certain name, but they didn't prepare you for life. I mean, what do you say when Howard Strickling (director of publicity) wasn't around . . . ?"

On May 18, 1921, with the purchase of Overlook Farm, ten miles west of Omaha, as future site of the Home, Father Flanagan realized his dream. His self-contained world, much as MGM was for Mayer, had Father Flanagan's personal vision written all over it. Its acreage, including a few buildings to be renovated, was a fantasy-come-true; the priest was establishing a singular, utopian home for unwanted and lost boys.

A few years later, Father Flanagan had orchestrated a beautiful campus into a state-of-the-art facility. His home was a prep school environment, complete with statuary, boulevards, playing fields, art centers, and training facilities, to go with church, dormitories, and administrative offices. With all haste Father Flanagan supervised a complete move to Overlook Farm and its subsequent development. The initial change of address was completed in October of 1921.

A decade ahead of the thinking at MGM, Father Flanagan decided on a weekly radio show to promote, to publicize, and to win support for his Home for Boys. In January of 1926 he began a weekly radio show, featuring the Boys' Home Band, each Monday at 6pm on WAOW, which could reach out to Nebraska and Wisconsin. The publicity machine at MGM would choose to do a weekly show in the mid-1930s, featuring radio re-enactments of new films with the original cast.

Lessons Father Flanagan learned from his media blitz led him to institute changes at his Boys Home. Within a month of the radio show, he held elections, allowing the boys to choose democratically a slate of councilors to have the ostensible responsibility of running the community. Resident boys promptly decided to change the name of Overlook Farm to Boys Town.

As MGM became renowned for its top-notch productions in the 1920s, due to Thalberg's contributions to several notable classics (*Ben Hur, The Big Parade*), Louis B. Mayer and his executive echelon formed a group referred to in the industry as the "College of Cardinals," and Mayer was the "pope." According to one B-movie star, "MGM had a caste system, just like India. Everybody had their position, and that position was important and it was also important that you realized your position."

Mayer and his Cardinals ran MGM's production line with their roles at the top of the chain of command. It was more difficult to reach Mayer, but the bureaucracy made the place run effectively. Mayer did not micromanage. Some continued to call Mayer vile names, while others saw him "a fascinating figure: brilliant, seductive, unprincipled, but all in all a man of genius."

Known as the Lion of Hollywood, according to biographer Scott Eyman's research, the studio was state of the art, down to the smallest details that Mayer approved. At the Commissary, he wanted the best dining experience, not merely to placate his creative workforce, but to keep them from straying from the studio at lunchtime, or if they were needed, later at night. Warners had the problem of stars dashing across the street to a local watering hole, only to return in worse condition. Louis B. Mayer forestalled that issue at Metro.

Using the design of Cedric Gibbons, his set designer emeritus, Mayer authorized a dining space to sit 225 people, in the most stunning *art deco* style of chrome and green. The Commissary's atmosphere, being modern and pleasant, its cuisine had to be of the highest quality available. MGM's commissary was famous for chefs catering to the idiosyncrasies and table favorites of its employees. Studio decorations on Fourth of July were now devoted to Mayer's birthday, tied gloriously to the celebration of American Independence. MGM held a surprise party each year for their leader, and the MGM orchestra played in the Commissary on special occasions.

Tables were reserved for directors, and others for the writers. Stars had specially prepared dishes, rare coffees, or whatever culinary delights that made them contented screen performers. Late work was not a problem, as the Commissary soon remained open twenty-four hours per day. A hub of the studio, its bulletin board announced golf tournaments and social gatherings. Mayer was instrumental in creating the counterpoint journalism of Hedda Hopper who shared political sympathy with Mayer and dropped any *bon mot* the studio wanted in print.

In addition, Mayer gave the actors a working environment that could not be matched at other studios. Offering customized dressing rooms and providing fresh flowers each day, MGM reeked of class. Writers, directors, and actors, toiled at other studios. At MGM, they savored the experience. Mayer strove to keep the studio self-sufficient. If anything was wanted, it could be brought to the vast lot. At Christmas Mayer had stores bring merchandise, so cast and crew didn't have to shop in public, and thus work with fewer interruptions or worries.

An assembly line of movies were scheduled, budgeted, and moved along briskly. Standard in-studio films were produced in forty-four days, while expensive and complicated movies, done with location shootings, were to be completed in fifty-nine days. Locations often were major headaches for crew, actors, and especially the producers.

After Irving Thalberg's death in 1936, fewer and fewer trips off the Metro lot were planned, and those scheduled were of shorter duration.

A major picture like *Captains Courageous* spent upwards of twenty weeks to be completed and ready for the movie houses. Whatever the quality, the problems such shoots encompassed became prohibitive. Contracted players were on call six days per week, for forty weeks per year. Three-month vacations were scheduled annually without pay, though salary was amortized for weekly paychecks.

Mayer dismissed the notion of stars being born. Though it might seem, he gave himself credit for the work, Louis B. Mayer was far more astute than to hog the limelight or to be a complete autocrat. "A star is made, created; carefully and cold bloodedly built up from nothing, from nobody. All I ever looked for was a face. If someone looked good to me, I'd have him tested. If a person looked good on film, if he photographed well, we could do the rest. Age, beauty, talent, least of all talent, had nothing to do with it."

The producer explained, "Once I saw a face that I liked . . . once I had the face, we could do the rest. It did not have to be a pretty face, nor even a handsome face . . . . If it were a face that I liked, I knew that the American people would like it too!" Mayer knew that his talent was to pass what he couldn't do over to experts and allow them free reign and creative control. "We hired geniuses at makeup, hair dressing, surgeons to slice away a bulge here and there. Rubbers to rub away the blubbers, clothes designers, lighting experts, coaches in everything."

In the dark days of the 1930s, Father Flanagan scoured newspapers for sensational news accounts of bad boys. He found one of his most controversial in August, 1931; Herbert Nichols—a twelve-year-old murderer in Walla Walla, Washington. Details of his case incensed Father Flanagan, and he raised a commotion about mistreatment of this boy. Appealing to the governor of Washington to insist the youngster should not go to prison or reformatory, Father Flanagan brought himself into national headlines. Herbert Nichols seemed to show all the signs of narcolepsy, a victim in the priest's perspective, not deserving of disposal in a maximum-security prison.

The governor of Washington attacked Flanagan's motives, and the priest with an unerring sense of injustice went after Governor and his untenable position. Their dispute over the boy guaranteed publicity and gave Flanagan the platform he wanted. Though he lost the case, he visited Nichols in prison—seeing him as sensitive and confused, housed with adult prisoners. If ever there was a crusade for Father Flanagan, this became it. His message reached every newspaper in America and gave him a celebrity Hollywood could not ignore.

Flanagan's philosophy flashed across the nation. There were no bad boys. In his world he saw boys as having inferiority complexes who think they can do nothing right. They merely needed some guidance and assurance. Father Flanagan wanted no stigma on his boys—hence, no uniforms, no incarcerations. To some a bleeding heart, Flanagan quickly developed into a kind of "Dear Abby." Parents throughout the nation wrote to him for advice on how to handle their problem children. Flanagan kept their addresses and created his appeal lists from these requests and fan letters. He was quick to jump on any device apt to bring in money for the town. His concept was a rehab center, resembling a home rather than an institution.

The cleric explained his categories of three kinds of boys: homeless, delinquent, and antisocial. He had strategies to identify and to help each type of adolescent. By 1932 this procedure and method attracted an average of nearly 300 boys per year to his home. There were several incorrigible boys who stayed with him for a time; each of these could easily be the role model for Mickey Rooney's character, Whitey Marsh, in the future movie. The first of these boys appeared as early as 1918. Flanagan identified their problems as a resentful to condescending and expressing a desire to be a big shot among boys. The arrogance had to be worked upon.

His home was a transitional place, preparation for a return to their actual families or a foster home. Many of Flanagan's methods, revolutionary in his day, now seem standard and common sense. He provided a large segment of his manuscript on his placement success. He gave foster parents advice on how to behave, and he believed in the importance of matching a boy to a suitable set of foster parents. He also allowed any boy who entered the home to tarry so long as they needed the succor of his town.

Father Flanagan said modestly he ran "a great railroad station." The achievements of Father Flanagan caught the eye of at least one producer at Metro-Goldwyn-Mayer. The priest and boy charges were the stuff of movie melodrama and attracted the attention of the America's most wholesome studio. Flanagan could not have been in better hands, for Mayer would present Boys Town exactly as the priest most desired.

One of Metro's big stars of the 1940s swimming musicals, Esther Williams observed: Louis B. Mayer "may have been an immigrant with a good suit of clothes, but never forget that this was a man working hard to be an American." This underscored by Katharine Hepburn who greatly respected the producer: "He adored the business, and he understood it." In her view Mayer was a romantic, a man who had extreme opinions about the goodness of the American culture. Ann Rutherford, of the popular Andy Hardy films stated: "He taught himself grammar. He taught himself manners. If anybody on earth ever created himself, Louis B. Mayer did."

Between the two giants and their special worlds, Boys Town and MGM, they created something new, unlike all others that came before and would come after. Each treated the individual with dignity and *esprit de corps* that bordered on a parallel to family. Though Mayer had his own opinions, he would listen to others and respected his producers. In the same manner Father Flanagan gave wayward boys a role in self-determination that made them responsible. By doing so, both institutions developed loyalty and trust among those who found a livelihood.

Time after time, and example after example, Flanagan and Mayer would have a coterie of followers who swore that these men gave them a chance to become someone special.

The bottom line was that Mayer knew how to make money and entertain people. For Flanagan money was necessary to feed and house homeless children and provide nurturing environment. In that way the difference between them remained monumental. Money was the tool to accomplish what they loved: to give something they believed lacking in society. Their rewards too were satisfying. Both disliked selfishness and cruelty to weaker folk.

Could the two men have reversed their lives? Might a Mayer have started a Boys Town? Could Flanagan have run a major film studio? Whether or not it's probable, the two men gave Americans in the 20th century a chance at their Constitutional right to happiness. Flanagan and Mayer pursued their dreams and led the world along with them.

2

MGM AND BOYS TOWN

Thought of as the studio's artistic conscience, producer and boy wonder Irving Thalberg also could be arrogant, and it cost Metro-Goldwyn-Mayer. In 1933 MGM paid damages to the living people depicted in the movie *Rasputin and the Empress*. An epic about the murder of the Russian mystic monk, it starred the Barrymore siblings—Ethel, Lionel, and John. However during the scripting, Irving Thalberg insisted on a scene in which Rasputin raped a young princess. The incident never really happened; the writer of the screenplay balked, warning Thalberg that the woman and her husband, on whom characters were based, were still alive, exposing the studio to legal action. Thalberg fired the writer and included the scene.

Soon as the movie was released, the outraged Russian princess on whom the character was based sued MGM in London and New York. The studio lost both suits, costing them $127,000 in England and a quick settlement of $250,000 in New York. The offending scene was cut from subsequent prints, and a new phrase joined the lexicon of all fictionalized writings: "The events and characters in this film are fictional, and any resemblance to characters living or dead is purely coincidental."

After that incident, MGM became gun-shy about the notion of biographical movies about living people. Perhaps it was the reluctance of MGM to tackle another movie whose subject was alive and active, but eager Father Flanagan wanted to have a film made about his work and home for boys, but not necessarily about himself. He was willing to publicize his program with an up-beat, first-class movie, and he supplied the studio with an unpublished manuscript, which described his ground-floor operation.

The priest had a history of nearly twenty years of service to the community; his background life story was basically public domain. Though he wanted a movie of his program, MGM or any other studio could film its own story about him without him by changing the names and fictionalizing all moments in the priest's life. Therefore, to satisfy legalities, Father Flanagan sold the rights to his life to MGM for $1 in 1935. A donation of $5,000 was also made to Boys Town much later, and Father Flanagan was told he would have script approval, as well as the right to accept or reject the finished film. This latter item was unheard of, and many in the industry still cannot believe a major studio of that era would agree to such a contractual clause.

The most interested producer on the Metro lot was John Considine, a burly Irish-descended member of the upper-echelon of the Mayer bigwigs. In the summer of 1937 John Considine sent his first team of researchers to Boys Town. This initial group included Eleanor Griffin, on whom the onus of the film script rested. Born in St. Paul, Minnesota, transplanted to MGM, she was one of many women who found a rosy future at Metro as a writer. She was accompanied to Omaha by fifty-year old O.O. Dull, Considine's associate producer and trusted aide.

The third member of the entourage was William Rankin, a writer who subsequently dropped from the team. Rankin's revenge was to go to RKO Studios where, ten years later, he wrote the script for Pat O'Brien's motion picture entitled *Fighting Father Dunne*, a movie about a priest in 1905 who began a shelter for newsboys in St. Louis. Dunne was a genuine precursor to Father Flanagan, and perhaps the inspiration for the larger and successful Boys Town that Flanagan envisioned for Omaha.

John Considine had a long and warm correspondence with Father Flanagan over several years, broaching the likelihood of a film about his retreat for young boys. It was through this series of letters that Father Flanagan probably began to toy with the idea of Spencer Tracy in the role of the priest, but dared not mention it. On June 28, 1937, Father Flanagan met Griffin, Dull, and Rankin, at his office on the Boys Town campus.

In a later interview given to the *Omaha World Herald*, Father Flanagan revealed he jumped at the chance to make the movie. The newspaper stated, "He would have been glad to have had the picture made with no payment to the home, so confident was he that the publicity would be a big help." His private feelings were another matter. In his mind the movie had no love story, and had no women in the cast. It seemed to his untrained eye, a recipe for disaster. He thought: "The movie people are old enough to know what they're doing."

During the initial talks between Flanagan and the delegation from MGM, the studio admitted they were not sure at this point what kind of picture would result. They suggested to the priest that there was the likelihood that the movie might even prove to become a "B (run of the mine) picture" in Monsignor Flanagan's own words.

Dull revealed to local media that the story was "a natural." He informed reporters he expected Mickey Rooney and Jackie Cooper would join Bartholomew as part of the cast of *Boys Town*, a new first-rate project. Dull also brought along an MGM 8mm movie camera to take pictures of the campus for Considine and the Art Department at Metro, indicating what might need to be replicated at the studio and what could only be photographed on location. At this point, no contracts or official business had been conducted beyond securing the rights to the story.

For nearly ten days, Miss Griffin led the team by interviewing boys and making case studies for possible plotlines. She also took still photographs, toured the facility, and met with Msgr. Flanagan. Though the village school had no dramatic arts program, there were boys who acted on the weekly radio program created by Father Flanagan.

These youngsters, led by their teacher, Adolph Brandes, began to think in terms of acting in the proposed motion picture. Eleanor Griffin also contributed to the idea that the visiting Metro team was searching for talent to play roles in the upcoming picture. This created a buzz among the boys that they might all have a chance to become movie stars.

Eleanor Griffin and Dull also hinted that most, if not all, of the motion picture would be filmed on location at Boys Town. To this idea, Father Flanagan offered a damper: "We're not going to have the film company disrupting our school schedule." This led Considine to consider filming during the summer when the school year was over.

For sixteen-year-old home resident Sam Turner, the film was potentially his big break. Though he did not have a chance to meet Eleanor Griffin, he told the *Omaha World Herald* that he was ready to play an extra or bit part. Two boys who worked on the radio broadcasts, Billy Kenny and John Gough, both thirteen, enjoyed a chance to converse with Eleanor Griffin who found them ideal types for her script.

Seven-year-old Jimmy Lang most inspired Griffin. Regarded as a Boys Town mascot, one of the youngest at the village, he was blond, blue-eyed, freckle-faced, and all-American. Jimmy idolized the current mayor of the town, Larry Kennedy, who had just been signed by the St. Louis Browns to pitch for their team. The friendship between Larry, called Butch, and Little Jimmy, impressed her and found its way into the initial script by Griffin.

The rights and story were in limbo until Thalberg, never well, died of heart failure in 1936. Under Thalberg, Metro was frequently seen as Retake Valley. If a film product was under his control, the finished picture might go through many rewrites, after shooting began. Thalberg always redid movies up to 25% of the footage.

If after a preview, it needed work, he insisted upon it, no matter what the cost. Not necessarily popular with the front office, nor Mayer, up to five years were used on a project that mattered. After Thalberg's death, this philosophy changed. Not only was a movie of Boys Town possible, it could be on a fast-track, unheard of at MGM up to that time.

When Eleanor Griffin, one of Considine's staff, began to whet the producer's interest in the subject of the orphan boy story, Considine chose to pursue it fully. After all, MGM had a bunch of moppets under contract, and the appetite in the public for stories about children had never been stronger.

Writing scripts at Metro was a chancy affair, depending on the producer assigned to supervise the writer's work. By 1935 Louis B. Mayer was barely speaking to Thalberg. "Each of them wanted what the other had," said Dore Schary, "Mayer, Thalberg's creative style and mind; Thalberg, Mayer's money and lusty power."

Another writer, unhappier than most, was Ring Larner, Jr., but confessed: "At Metro, you never thought that Mayer looked at scripts. At Metro you worked with a producer. At Fox you had a producer, but everybody was waiting to see what Zanuck would say. At Metro producers had a lot more say."

The job of writing scripts took place under top-notch working conditions. At MGM, according to Dore Schary, "MGM's Administration

Building, four stories of white concrete set in green lawn, is located at the east end of the production lot and is known because of its air-conditioning system as the Iron Lung. In its four hundred offices are housed the company executives, the lawyers, the several producers, the writers, and 'Story Department'.

Schary considered John Considine brilliant at his job. "The germ ideas which grow into motion pictures are often very simple. Usually they can be expressed in the length of a telegram. And usually they come from simple beginnings. The trick is to recognize them."

This was something Considine proved with the Boys Town storyline. He was the first at MGM to see its possibilities. Thalberg was now gone from the scene, giving the producer latitude to pursue his individual approach to the topic. "The starting point of a story, any story is somebody's idea; a germ idea which somebody considers promising enough to justify the effort of filling and fleshing and building it out into a form ready for the public's judgment."

At Metro in 1936, the reigning storylines put a focus on child stars. They were the public's darlings, and MGM had two of the most popular children on their contracted players roll: Freddie Bartholomew and Mickey Rooney. In Eleanor Griffin's original story, children were meant to be the focus, not Father Flanagan.

According to a *New York Times* piece in 1938: "Successful child stars are not individuals; they are industries. Of all the strange lives fashioned by a fantastic town, those of celluloid moppets are the most grotesque. In a few brief years, if they capture the public's fancy, they receive fortunes, which, in more normal walks of life, successful adults must struggle for decades to attain. They not only enrich their parents but they bring affluence to all those identified with them."

Eleanor Griffin saw herself as writing a follow-up to the *Captains Courageous* movie, reuniting Bartholomew and Rooney, two of the scant few making the big bucks. Young Freddie was the hottest boy on the Metro lot, making at least $2000 per week with an involved series of bonuses. "Mickey Rooney, one of the most consistent money-makers among the juveniles, earns $750 a week at Metro; if he last this will reach $2000 at the end of seven years." The Andy Hardy movies were catapulting him beyond Bartholomew. Rooney would make $2000 every week before two years passed.

Considine's writer went through the material sent to her. She noted Father Flanagan's comment in his manuscript: "I decided to go after the saplings . . ." This was an intriguing idea during the rage of moppet movies of the 1930s. Eleanor Griffin envisioned a plot about the first mayor of Boys Town allegedly winning his race with a bribe of Christmas candy to voters in a community where the worst punishment inflicted was to be forced to watch the week's scheduled movie with one's back to the movie screen.

Father Flanagan made mention of a dog mascot at Boys Town. The animal, named Hector by some and Carlo by others, was rescued by the original boys from the streets of Omaha and adopted by them. He lived to a ripe old age. Hector (or Carlo) upon death went to a taxidermist at the resident boys' insistence. The stuffed mascot then became threadbare thin as boys rubbed his fur for good luck over the years. The dog story element also inspired the screenwriter with its sentimental appeal.

Flanagan had done all this work without support from any church, government agency, or community chest, further adding to typical material sought for an MGM family film.

The pages of Father Flanagan's manuscript provided the gist of the movie, as he supplied a narrative of a typical day at Boys Town. Having to produce a script that pleased the priest, Griffin read the cleric's chronology of life for the boys carefully and extracted key details for her synopsis.

Interviewed during a preliminary visit by MGM producers to Boys town, teacher Adolph Brandes and his students thought movie roles would be available for them. Photo courtesy of Omaha World Tribune.

The priest recounted in his manuscript that by the mid-1930s, Father Flanagan's Boys Home had transformed into a legitimate town, incorporated by the state in 1936; they had been given their own post office and postal code. By-laws of the state allowed them to hold valid elections for mayor and councilors. Voting age was seven.

A bugle sounded at 6am each morning to signal the start of the day. Mass or other religious services were optional, but exercise was recommended. By 7am there was breakfast. It was like a dining hall rather than a cafeteria. Eight boys sat at a table, and boys took turns as wait-staff who served the others. It wasn't the MGM Commissary, but for boys who sometimes never had regular meals, it was just as heavenly. Breakfast lasted about half an hour; then duties were assigned.

School began at 8:30 and the primary objective of the curriculum was, in Father Flanagan's words, "learning how to be a man." Most boys were in the junior high school range to the first year of high school. They offered two years of high school at first. Manual training was a central offering, as well as carpentry and other skills. An apprentice class in sculpting opened in the 1930s as well as a laundry shop, and tailor training, new subjects possible at the old Overlook Farm, now transformed. Agricultural studies were extremely popular with many of the Midwestern, farm-raised boys. They operated a cannery and put up supplies for the winter; flocks of 2000 chicks to feed and to care for were assigned to individual boys.

Father Flanagan sought out those showing secretarial and editorial skills as his office aides. These personal assistants, as he called them, did all his correspondence and office work. He also started a print shop for his monthly journal.

A bugle sounded lunch at noon every day.

Father Flanagan stressed the importance of extracurricular activities. Three music bands, based on advancement and talent playing instruments, were formed. Twenty-eight boys were assigned to each band. Flanagan stipulated no school uniforms at Boys Town. His boys wore overalls mostly, using things like colored belts to express individuality. On Sundays the traditionalist priest preferred suits and ties.

Extremely popular seasonal sports were offered. When listing sports, Father Flanagan's priority was: "Football, boxing, basketball, track, baseball, tennis, marbles." The priest actually preferred boxing, and early photographs indicated many boys agreed with him. Teams were formed by age. A swimming pool was also installed in the 1930s, well before the movie, and Flanagan called it the "finest athletic investment." Rows of showers in the shower room also doubled as the bathing facility for the boys.

For special recreation and shows, there was an auditorium and movie house at Boys Town. Flanagan allowed only family wholesome films (most similar to the L.B. Mayer philosophy). Boys tended to prefer adventure stories like *Captains Courageous*, family fare like Andy Hardy, or Abbott and Costello programmers. Evening entertainments included Amateur talent nights, usually on Friday or Saturday.

At 7pm Flanagan supervised a downtime. The "quiet time" was one in which he personally supervised each day as a time for intimate conversations with boys. This enhanced his One Big Family concept. This was a condition that kept the priest in touch with the daily issues at Boys Town. At 8pm, the boys prepared for bed.

Each day there were constant comings and goings of new boys and old boys. Former residents remained in contact with Father Flanagan. Letters from them about their progress was important to the priest for their welfare and for evidence of the success of his program. He also used them for fund raising purposes. By 1934, the time of his manuscript, he had registered 4500 boys though his doors.

One of his few favorites was a boy named Henry in the manuscript, nicknamed Pinky, owing to his reddish blond hair. Because the cleric made many "show trips," Flanagan sought out certain boys with fine speaking voices and highly presentable to accompany him across the country on various speaking engagements to raise funds.

Father Flanagan's dream for the future was to have Boys Town grow more and more, never to become static. He wanted to increase "whenever and however this may be accomplished." He desired an institution that paralleled a "congenial family." Many times in his manuscript he insisted that "we must educate the heart and the soul," and "who can say what a boy is worth?"

Among the bits of research Eleanor Griffin consulted in her file at MGM was a souvenir book, produced in 1935 by the Boys Town Press. It was one of many pamphlet style booklets the priest used to inform the public about his creation and to solicit donations. Miss Griffin read that on Oct. 19, 1930, Father Flanagan went forward with plans to build four new buildings to house the boys and to give them some activities space. Gov. Arthur J. Weaver of Nebraska on Dec. 5, 1934, oversaw the dedication of a new post office.

Boys Town was made an official town of the state. Soon after it had a mayor and six commissioners. First election for mayor was held in January, 1935. These were real elections, and there was a two party system. BBT and HOTS were acronyms, standing for Build Better Boys and Help Our Town. Commissioners of the community included police, buildings, public works, parks and grounds, public safety, and health.

Famous visitors continued to call at Boys Town, including generous supporters like Will Rogers and Admiral Richard E. Byrd who spent his forty-seventh birthday at Boys Town in 1935. Photographs of the priest with such celebrities were routinely printed in nationally syndicated newspapers.

The first MGM synopsis for Boys Town was dated May 26, 1937, for which the studio's Story Department authorized an eight-page summary. In reality it was a sales pitch to prove the subject was worthy of an MGM script and production. In the initial version, the priest's establishment was called an unusual 'character factory', containing the physical plant, then worth in excess of $1 million for over dozens of acres and eleven buildings. In testimony to the worthiness of the subject for a movie, MGM measured Boys Town by its fiscal soundness.

Dore Schary observed, "There is no such thing as a typical screen writer," and the variety of proposed film scripts about Boys Town surely proved him right. The first step in the process of making a film was to have a writer create a screen treatment for the producer.

In one of his books about the movie business, Schary explained: "The treatment is simply a rough sketch of the proposed picture: most screen originals which we buy for filming are in treatment form. Screen writers are constantly being asked by outside writers just how a treatment should be set up, the fact is, there is no form: you simply tell the story."

Treatments at Metro were expected to be the fewest number of pages needed to clearly state the storyline and to show how the tale might interest viewers. Sharply delineated characters had to move the story straight to its climax. A good treatment revealed major characters' actions and reactions and stressed its most visual moments and scenes. Schary insisted the writer "must find ways to introduce his important people characteristically and memorably without being obvious about it . . ." Writers should "invent brief transitions to take the place of lengthy dull sequences. Everything the screenwriter does must test against two standards: the words "simple" and "inevitable.""

The earliest plot attempts for Boys Town rambled about and did little of this.

3

THE STORY OF MANY SCRIPTS

After the release of *Captains Courageous* in May of 1937, MGM came to the realization they had one of the best films ever made on their hands. Its universal praise convinced the studio that it was a major hit, and the desire to replicate it was expressed to contracted writers by producers.

Months later, when Oscar nominations were announced, this frenzy to produce something akin to the Kipling yarn grew stronger. There were rumors a film property for Mickey Rooney and Freddie Bartholomew might be in the works.

The first MGM treatment for a Boys Town movie came at the beginning of June in 1937. Almost two months later, at the end of July, Eleanor Griffin had her forty-five-page treatment ready for the production office and John Considine.

One *motif* put into the story was a trinket given to Father Flanagan by Skinny. It was a pocket toy with the face of a tiger with two tiny silver ball bearings needing to be rolled into the little grooves of the tiger's eyes. This plot device was used regularly throughout the movie, to allay the priest's stress, or as an item he would sell to his benefactor, Dave, for a cash advance to improve the home for the boys.

Griffin's initial version of the story focused entirely on the first five boys and efforts to save them. This was a moppet movie wherein Father Flanagan was simply a secondary figure, given the fictional name of Father Mulcahy.

The five boys taken into the original home became the major characters. Lefty and Petie, were the key roles of the group. The story began in 1925, not the historically accurate 1917. The pawnbroker friend was named Dave Morris and was a central foil and catalyst for the priest's home. One line at the end was notable, "Kin you come back to the home?" Asked of Father Mulcahy, he responded incredulously to the wayward runaway boy: "There will be a brass band waiting for you!"

Griffin received the approval to proceed, but at the same time as she was writing the full script, she received word of a fire at Boys Town. The storage facility with all the winter cloaks and coats mysteriously caught fire and was totally destroyed. Her movie script topped out at 99 pages and was complete on August 16, 1937, not long after returning from her two-week stint visiting Omaha.

Eleanor Griffin altered several things after that visit; the name Mulcahy was crossed out during the first 14 pages and the name Flanagan was hand-written into the script. Beyond her prologue pages, the new name for the priest's role was typed in as Father Flanagan.

Considine and MGM had been thinking along the same lines after the Oscar nomination Tracy got for playing a priest in San Francisco. The recent teaming with Freddie Bartholomew required a story in which Tracy could again interact with his latest co-star in a new picture.

MGM may have harbored some thoughts of doing the Boys Town story without Flanagan's approval, but having bought his rights for $1, the studio could choose to make the film as a tribute to Flanagan after all. The trip to the facility altered the commitment of the studio. Father Flanagan signed a contract with MGM in mid-July, 1937, indicating his support of the project. Though he was invited to be technical advisor on the picture, news reports stating that he performed this task were incorrect.

Metamorphosing occurred in the script; the character of Petie in the earlier version was now called Skinny. Dave, openly called a Jew in the dialogue, remained the key donor to Boys Town in the next script. One of the other boys became Mickey Ryan (clearly the Mickey Rooney character of the future). It may well be that the role was now written for the up and coming star, Rooney, to play. The brash lines and personality were clearly a prototype of Whitey Marsh.

This script contained the first attempt of the reclamation of Mickey's character. Here, he was hostile to the orphan home dog, named Butch (not the real name of Hector). However as the facility burned down, Mickey Ryan rushed into the flame-covered building to save the animal—to the everlasting gratitude of all the other boys and Father Flanagan.

This first complete script placed growing emphasis on the priest, changing the earlier treatment, but he was still a featured character, not the central focus. The script won approval by producers John Meehan and John Considine for consideration as a film project. A snag of some sort occurred. Still a year away from the actual production, the script about Boys Town was discarded. A new outline and attempt was authorized.

It remained unclear if Father Flanagan declined to accept that storyline. According to Dore Schary, Father Flanagan was a hard man to please with scripts, and most of the early ones were put aside because of his objections.

At this point producer John Considine ordered two major script drafts prepared about Boys Town by different scriptwriters on the Metro lot. First, Brad Foote began his synopsis of the story. Working simultaneously, Walter Wise and Hugo Butler presented their treatment of the Flanagan story two days after Bradford Foote's version. Eleanor Griffin's work was still the basis for these drafts. Several ideas of hers remained viable in every script to follow.

Wise, on staff since 1936, had written a few shorts; this was a big project for him. Butler's future was both rosy and horrible. He was later nominated for an Oscar in 1940 for writing another Tracy role in *Edison The Man*, and then was blacklisted in the 1950s as un-American and moved to Mexico for thirteen years, dying of a heart attack at age 53.

Dated October 5, 1937, a new four-page outline emerged, done by Bradbury Foote. This plot synopsis bore many scenes and moments that survived until the finished movie script. There were extraordinary anomalies to the film everyone recalls so fondly.

Mickey Ryan was the main protagonist and focus of the storyline, having his ties to a bank robber named John Loomis. Mickey remained unrepentant and had conflicts with other boys as well as Father Flanagan. Butch the dog was still a central plot device. This time the dog was killed in a car accident when he crossed the street, chasing after Mickey who had dismissed the dog's love and loyalty.

Distraught and desperate, Mickey rejoined his criminal pals who become involved in another bank holdup where a guard was killed, but Mickey was innocent of the bank robbery where he became involved when merely trying to protect Loomis.

Eventually caught and about to be thrown into the official prison system, he enjoyed an important supporter in Father Flanagan who wanted to take him to Boys Town and was willing to stake his reputation that Mickey was not a bad boy. The courts refused to accept this and forced a trial with Mickey as defendant.

Tried as an adult, Mickey felt overwhelmed with the adult world. During this crisis, Father Flanagan must go to court to prove Mickey was not a bad boy. Thinking this as only way to validate his mission, Father Flanagan delivered a stirring courtroom declaration that won Mickey's exoneration. Though he succeeded on this, afterward, Father Flanagan was injured and hospitalized because of a fire at Boys Town. All ended well in this screenplay. Flanagan fully recovered, and Mickey was unanimously elected Police Commissioner of Boys Town.

Bradbury Foote's best years were at Metro from 1938 to 1941 when he worked on scripts for *Young Tom Edison*, *Billy the Kid* and Mickey Rooney's *Hold that Kiss*. He also faded from Hollywood during that Blacklist period, but lived to age 101, dying in 1995.

The Wise-Butler treatment was offered to producer John Considine on October 7, 1937. This version avoided any prologue or explanation on how Boys Town was founded by Father Flanagan, though it was made clear to the audience through scene dialogue that he had borrowed $5000 from Dave Morris, his pawnbroker friend for improvements to the Home for Boys.

Mickey Ryan remained a key figure in this storyline, referred to as a 13-year-old bank robber who challenged Flanagan's concept of good being in every boy. A classic problem child, the boy resisted the moral environment of Boys Town and the influence of his peers. He instigated an arch-rivalry with Petie, the mayor.

Nonetheless, Butch the dog took a liking to Mickey, when no one else except Father Flanagan had sympathy for him. He also clashed and spoke angry words with Cohn, a Jewish boy who was the barber at Boys Town.

Despite the faith of Father Flanagan in him, Mickey stood accused (but falsely) of the bank robbery charge, and the founder of Boys Town went to court to defend his charge. When they returned to Boys Town, after having Father Flanagan save Mickey during an impassioned plea in court, Butch the dog was hit by a car on the highway to Boys Town, testing the faith and love of the residents. There was also a fire at Boys Town in which the priest suffered injury while saving his boys. Father Flanagan recovered from hospitalization, and all's well in the final reel when Flanagan was elected 1937's Citizen of the Year.

On October 26, 1937, just a few days after the Roman Catholic Church diocese of Omaha elevated Father Edward Flanagan to the position of Monsignor, Wise and Butler wrote a full treatment for their ideas. It now evolved into a reunion of the young stars of the blockbuster *Captains Courageous*. The role of Father Flanagan, continuing to be secondary in the script, was not then being openly mentioned for any of the usual Metro players.

Walter Brennan, so identified in the script, was to portray an older, bank-robbing mentor to two boys called Mickey (Rooney) and Limey (Freddie Bartholomew). The British boy, Limey, was identified as the orphan son of a British family whose sister lived in Nebraska and with whom he resided.

Mickey and Limey began a life of delinquent behavior and crime by robbing a local store. There was no Flanagan prologue to the movie script, nor any establishing shots of Boys Town. The story centered on the two boys as the main engine of the plot. During one of their heists Mickey was caught by police and sent to jail. L

Limey was remanded to the custody of Father Flanagan, where at Boys Town he met Little Petie and then became mayor through his hard work. Proving worthy of Father Flanagan's style of rehabilitation, Limey often led the community of boys in grace at dinner, and he developed into a model citizen under Father Flanagan's tutelage.

In contrast, the parallel story had Mickey beaten up in Reform School, living under terrible conditions. Much as went right for Limey, life was unfair and cruel for Mickey, who got increasingly incorrigible and resentful. Father Flanagan managed to rescue Mickey and took him back to Boys Town.

Limey and Father Flanagan attempted kindness and sympathy to undo the horrors of prison life. Mickey proved to be nearly impossible to reach, and he terminated his stay at Boys Town by running off to rejoin the gang led by Walter Brennan.

Out of loyalty to his friend, Limey followed him as he ran away. He tried to talk him out of rejoining his old criminal associates. Mickey refused to listen and was involved in a shooting. Limey, while trying to help him, was the one caught by the police and blamed for the crime. Mickey returned to Boys Town and Limey was put in jail. Mickey's conscience bugged him. When he wanted to confess to Father Flanagan about Limey's innocence, Boys Town became engulfed by fire.

Mickey went heroically into the flames to help others out of the building and was severely hurt. Father Flanagan rescued him. Fearing he was about to die, lying in the priest's arms, Mickey revealed Limey had nothing to do with the shooting or the robbery. Vindicated by Mickey's new attitude, Father Flanagan was successful in his defense of the boys, and all resumed life again at Boys Town.

Bradbury Foote gave it another try at the end of November. His outline, dated Nov. 29, 1937, was a scant ten pages. He also seemed to have word that Freddie Bartholomew and Mickey Rooney would be the stars. The script was tailored to meet their particular talents, while Father Flanagan was elevated to a stronger role in this new version of the story.

The screenplay opened in a contemporary Boys Town with a board meeting led by Father Flanagan in which he espoused some of his philosophy for child rearing. Boys Town was to be shown as complete, solvent, and an ideal rural atmosphere for boys. On this bucolic scene arrived a British boy (Bartholomew), son of a notorious British criminal. The boy was arrogant, hostile, and wanted to return to London.

At Boys Town, the British boy named Bayard or Bay met Nicky Peters (Mickey Rooney), the hard working mayor. From the start there was animosity and contempt from Bayard Blake toward the stalwart Nicky. Left alone in Father Flanagan's office, Bay stole $300 from the cash-strapped community. Soon it was clear a kleptomaniac was loose in the community. Many items were shown stolen by an unseen culprit. The boy, Bayard, was doing this to impress his father that he was cut from the same mold and was worthy of joining his father's gang.

Bay Blake then ran away to rejoin his father at a secret location. Unknown to him, Nick Peters followed him. When Bay arrived at his father's, he was not welcomed. Denounced as an ingrate, he got dismissed. Crying and rejected, Bay fell into Nick's arms, devastated. Back at Boys Town, Bay was despondent, depressed and spiritless. All the things previously stolen were returned item by item, and just as mysteriously.

In an attempt to bolster the psychological state of his friend, Nick Peters convinced Bay to run for mayor, and he sacrificed himself, by losing, to bolster his friend's fragile ego. At the same time, Bay's father had been caught by police and faced execution by electric chair. Father Flanagan took Bay to see his father at the state penitentiary, but the boy hid while Father Flanagan talked to Bayard's father who again ridiculed his son before being taken away. When Bay came out, the priest pointed out to Bay that, "you have worshipped a false god." Thus, Bay, Nick, and Father Flanagan, were happily reunited at Boys Town.

Scriptwriter Dore Schary was one of many who attempted to write a screenplay. Schary succeeded in his task, winning an Oscar—and later became head of Metro Goldwyn Mayer. Photo from author's collection.

Someone at MGM or, perhaps, Father Flanagan himself rejected this synopsis. Dore Schary believed it traced back to the priest, who was extremely concerned for the right image and story to represent his community. Boys Town suffered in the Great Depression, as did most of America. It was on shaky ground, nearly closing its doors at the height of the troubled 1930s. Father Flanagan needed a movie to keep his home for boys in the public eye. It was John Considine who informed Schary the priest rejected numerous treatments and screenplays, wanting the best movie possible for his Boys Town.

Dore had just returned from New York, where one of his plays, *Too Many Heroes*, opened to so-so reviews, but he kept that information to himself, leaving most at the studio to assume he penned a Broadway hit. "After reading what had been written and studying the history of Father Flanagan's unique institution, I told John Considine that the error holding up the project was the casting of Freddie Bartholomew in an atmosphere where he clearly did not belong."

Dore respected Considine, but was accountable to Harry Rapf, a dour man whose political situation at the studio may have contributed to his demeanor. Rapf fired Schary twice, and both times John Considine rehired the beleaguered writer. Eventually, Considine assigned Schary the important job of satisfying Father Flanagan with a storyline about Boys Town.

Considine fulfilled Schary's view of what a real Hollywood producer must be: "The term producer has many meanings in Hollywood. I will be talking here about only the real producers, the men who truly contribute to their pictures and to the industry, who try to do a job rather than hold one. In essence, a producer is a man who starts with an idea or hope and ends with a completed picture ready for the screen."

Shortly before Christmas, 1937, Dore began his own film treatment of the Flanagan story. As with most screenplays, writers are reluctant to jettison every detail. "Although there is no such thing as a sure fire picture, a fact which the industry rediscovers expensively at intervals, the outlook for most pictures can be estimated in the light of our experience with past pictures of the same type." He kept the concept of a Mickey Rooney storyline. This was a picture about a bad boy who must find redemption; Father Flanagan may have been the catalyst for this change, but Schary knew the box-office demanded that Mickey Rooney dominate the film story.

The task had devoured a number of writers during the past year, but Schary managed in less than three weeks to put together an eighty-page script for submission to John Considine. Schary completed the full script on Jan. 6, 1938. Once again, this story began with a Mickey Rooney scene, as the Flanagan role was beefed up but yet secondary and Tracy had not been approached to do the role.

The plot retained the concept of the kid brother of Marsh, a notorious criminal. At the outset, Father Flanagan, having agreed to take charge of the wayward youth named Whitey, visited him in his cold-water flat. The famous four-movement encounter was here completely intact. The priest removed Whitey's hat, pulled the cigarette from his mouth, yanked him up by his lapels, and sat down comfortably. It also featured Whitey falling to the floor, feigning injury, "You broke my arm." Taken to Boys Town, Whitey met the mayor, Petie Fuller, his nemesis, and Pee Wee, the waif mascot of Father Flanagan. Also here was Mo Kahn, the barber of Boys Town. These characters were fully developed.

In flashback there was a discussion of the roots of the Boys Home, the early vision of Father Flanagan with his tiger-eyes toy from Skinny, and a fateful meeting with Dave Morris. This version was an attempt to placate the cleric's philosophy by having Whitey visit a professor of psychology who represented what the Boys Town conception of assistance rejected. Also included was the bad haircut by given Mo Kahn, resulting in his fight with Whitey, and their punishment of standing with backs to the movie of the week.

Whitey and Petie clashed, and Whitey chose to run for mayor with the support of Mo and Pee Wee. Whitey's loss led to his confrontation with Petie in the boxing ring, refereed by Father Flanagan, another sop to the priest's interest in boxing as a teaching tool for boys. When Whitey lost, he abruptly left Boys Town, followed by a beseeching Pee Wee, not a dog, who was hit by a car when he dashed across a street chasing Whitey Marsh, who then cried out, "If we ever get out of this mess, I'll carry that kid on my back for the rest of my life."

During a prayer scene in which all of Boys Town was on its knees, appealing to God to help Pee Wee, Whitey ran off to Omaha where he reconnected with his brother, only to be involved in a planned bank robbery. A guard was killed this time, and Whitey was captured, to face trial for murder. Father Flanagan was determined to must save Whitey, whom he knew to be innocent.

At the climax of the trial, Flanagan delivered a speech about "let's learn about charity," and the eloquence of the priest won over the jury. The day was saved, and Whitey returned to Boys Town, reformed, and with the help of a healthy Pee Wee was quickly elected the new mayor.

In a coda, Whitey greeted a new boy, cocky as he once was. The kid chimed arrogantly, "Hiya, punk." Whitey winked at Father Flanagan, as they recognized the cycle had begun again.

Producer John Considine recognized the short screenplay draft was the best written so far and likely to win the approval of Father Flanagan. He asked Schary to make a personal visit to Boys Town, to offer the script to Father Flanagan, and win his support, if not approval. They'd already become acquainted when the writer and Jack Ruben were there to scout the village; in Considine's mind the professorial Dore was exactly the man for the job.

Leaving the warm weather of Southern California, Dore Schary had a bit of a shock when he arrived in Omaha. This time, he got the brunt of a bitter cold Nebraska winter. Ushered into Father Flanagan's office, writer had arrived by rented car in a near frozen state.

The cleric's welcoming smile defrosted him. Dore immediately handed him the script, which the priest glanced through briefly before placing it on his desk. He "joined me in a moment or two and relieved my chill and my tensions by offering a long drink of straight Irish whiskey. After we each had two of these generous appetizers, I was warm and captivated by the tall, craggy priest who spoke with a slight brogue, but with no affectation." Having settled on chairs comfortably, Dore commented on Nebraska's arctic temperature, but Father Flanagan was eager to read his script.

"He told me that the weather might be milder the next day, but for that night we would just have dinner together and talk."

They shared a cozy dinner, and Dore was advised to be careful driving the icy road and to get some rest, the priest seeing him out the door with script already in hand.

Returning to the Fontenelle Hotel that night, Schary worked on his notes. He spent two or three hours making outlines of his impressions of this unusual priest. Only one issue had emerged from the discussion that rattled Schary. Father Flanagan made an observation that surprised the writer.

Because of the proximity of the Oscar awards, the priest expressed an interest in having Spencer Tracy playing the role of Father Flanagan in the picture, knowing that Tracy had previously played a priest in the Clark Gable action drama, *San Francisco*, a year earlier. Tracy being a current Oscar nominee for *Captains Courageous*, publicity about him would have prodded Father Flanagan to suggest the star actor.

As originally envisioned, the role was hardly suitable for an Oscar winner, and not important enough in the script to sustain the interest of MGM's major film star. In an effort to bond with the priest, Dore agreed Tracy was an excellent choice, and was fully certain Tracy could portray Flanagan easily because "he had Tracy's charm, his smile and twinkle. He was going to be a cinch to catch on film." The dinner discussion inspired the writer to make Father Flanagan the main character in the screenplay; his script could evolve into a biographical picture about a man committed to goodness and benevolence.

He'd have to alert John Considine to this new wrinkle in the project. Tracy could not possibly be expected to play a supporting role in a Mickey Rooney picture—but might if the role was restructured into the leading one. Dore realized that single change would give the movie far more potential, "A property is greater because of Spencer Tracy."

4

TRACY AND ROONEY

As Dore Schary knew, sixty percent of all movie tickets sold in the heyday of movies, the 1930s and 1940s, were sold by star power. Studios used the star system because the public demanded it. Yet, the star must show, in Schary's words, "that indefinable twist of personality that jumps of the screen and takes hold of you. Nothing we can do will make the public buy tickets to a picture."

Spencer Tracy had it, yet lacked confidence to believe the public loved him and respected him. When Tracy was cast as a cleric in San Francisco, he said: "I had a tough time deciding whether or not to get myself out of the part. I thought of how my father wanted me to be a priest, and I wondered if it would be sacrilegious for me to play a priest. All of my Catholic training and background rolled around in my head, but then I figured Dad would have liked it, and I threw myself into the role."

Others at Metro were not pleased about W.S. Van Dyke's decision to cast Tracy as the pious friend of Clark Gable. They'd been giving him a sex appeal build up, but Tracy was "thrilled," according to Katharine Hepburn. The role gave him a chance to sink his teeth into a Grade-A MGM epic. In his journal, Tracy later wrote how he "got away with murder," on the set, referring to his scene stealing. His performance won him an Oscar nomination in 1936, and it also made him a star.

Louis B. Mayer was particularly proud of his star system, and he took full credit for discovering the actor, nurturing, and creating a draw who was among MGM's biggest. "Fox had him playing villains, and he probably would never have been anything more than a good character actor if I hadn't seen something wonderful about his face, something more important than his acting ability. We signed him, found just the right stories for him and he became Spencer Tracy, the star, not Spencer Tracy, the actor. We did that, no drama school did. We did it with the stories we picked for him, with cameras and lights and music and a hundred tricks."

In terms of his performance in *Captains Courageous*, as a doomed Portuguese fisherman, Tracy recorded in his journal, "best picture ever made," and that was the consensus among the industry and the public. He spent twenty weeks on this film, "with no time off," but he considered it the "best part ever too."

The Academy of Motion Pictures gave their Oscars on March 10, 1938. Spencer Tracy did not attend the ceremony where he was awarded Best Actor to thunderous applause in the auditorium. According to a few reports, he was hospitalized for a hernia operation. Others were less kind, saying alcohol-related problems kept him from the Ambassador Hotel in Los Angeles. In his journal, always brief and succinct, Tracy referred to having an infection in late February. It could have been possible that he was indeed recuperating from illness, not an alcoholic blackout, as many sources suggest.

In early March, John Considine put John Meehan and Schary to work on revising the screenplay of *Boys Town*. It had a new, important focus. Flanagan, not the boys, would be the centerpiece of the story. To accomplish this goal, Meehan and Schary returned to the original work of Eleanor Griffin. Considine wanted to merge her story of the roots of the original Home for Boys with the later tale Schary developed about the most incorrigible boy Father Flanagan ever met.

Eleanor Griffin sent a copy of the September, 1937, issue of the *Boys Town Newsletter* over to Dore for study. This was the original publication from Nebraska containing a picture of a six year old (Jimmy Lang) asleep on a chair in Flanagan's office as he worked nearby. He resembled the Pee Wee character in the film to come. Schary read of the barn-burning incident during the previous summer, but long ago jettisoned that hoary chestnut as a plot device.

Griffin underlined a passage for Schary. Eleanor pointed out a depressed line spoken by one lonely boy that Father Flanagan tried to reach: "Well, what if you do send me to reform school? Nobody would care anyhow." She wrote in margin in ink: "a very good line for the boy in court at end of our prologue!"

At this juncture, John Meehan began the intricate process of merging two disparate scripts with two over-arching characters, Father Flanagan and the fictional Dave Morris, a pawnbroker. The two halves were not seamless, but John Considine was moving quickly. Two years earlier, under Irving Thalberg, something like this would never have occurred.

"Extremely pleased," was how Schary described his producer. Considine sent the writer back to Boys Town two weeks later for continued research and discussion with Father Flanagan. For good measure, the producer asked his planned director to go along. J. Walter Ruben was commissioned to scout the locations. Ruben had worked at RKO for a while, but scored a recent big success by directing Jean Harlow, Spencer Tracy, and Mickey Rooney, in Riff Raff. He had promise and worked well with the two stars Considine had in mind for *Boys Town*.

Shary and Ruben visited every aspect of the village, and its winning basketball team truly impressed the Hollywood duo. They noted the team uniforms were in tatters. A call to Eddie Mannix, the general manager of MGM, corrected the problem. Authorized by the studio, the visitors bought new uniforms, equipment, and sneakers, through a sports outlet in Omaha.

By the time the uniforms were ready, Schary was back in California. A report came in to inform him the village team lost their first game while wearing their new finery. "I called Father Flanagan to extend my condolences," said Dore. "But he assured me that within a couple of games the uniforms would be dirty and torn once more and the boys would resume winning."

Numerous changes emerged as the script became centered on Father Flanagan. A flashback revealing how the Home started grew into a lengthy prologue. All of the original material of the Eleanor Griffin screenplay was back, featuring Skinny and his brother. Focus was placed on Dave Morris, the pawnbroker and investor in the early days of Father Flanagan's plan.

The story opened with Father Flanagan realizing that young boys, rather than grown men, required his help and were malleable to teaching and assistance. Once the Home became bigger, the original five boys merged with the growing crowd.

After the introduction of belligerent Whitey on his initial trip to Boys Town, the script presented a tour of the facility to show its state-of-the-art campus. The robbery scene in which Whitey was wounded was altered to tie in the capture of Whitey's brother with his bank robbery gang at the climax of the tale.

Another character named Tony Ponessa, a crippled boy, was added, fully developed, and Petie Fuller became Freddie Fuller, mayor of Boys Town. Cohn became Mo Kahn. Screen time increased for the Pee Wee character, and lesser dollops of dialogue made Freddie and Kahn minor characters. The role of Dave Morris as donor to the cause of the town expanded and became a motif comic foil to Father Flanagan.

Schary condensed his own script, removing or altering scenes that gave Whitey Marsh attention and emphasis. He was a catalyst of the second half, but shared his storyline with Father Flanagan. This script was now the story of the founder of Boys Town along with a depiction of its young residents.

Jimmy Lang was the youngest resident at Boys Town in 1937. He inspired writer Eleanor Griffin to create the character that later became Pee Wee, played by Bobs Watson. Photo courtesy of Omaha World Tribune.

Devastating news was give to Schary in April. Jack Ruben was diagnosed with an inflammation of the lining of his heart. It was a frightful trauma in light of the recent death of Irving Thalberg eighteen months earlier. Medical treatment at the time decreed complete rest for Jack Ruben. He had to withdraw from directing his first major film. For a full year he did little work, and only then as a producer on smaller productions. He was completely off the *Boys Town* movie. His condition stabilized for a few years, but in September of 1942, he succumbed to heart disease.

Troubles were just beginning for John Considine. When he approached Tracy with the idea of playing Father Flanagan, the star was evasive. Tracy, temperamental when it came to new film roles, was known to resist for a time, then came to grips with the part and gave a top-notch performance. As Schary revealed in his own autobiography, "After some weeks of stalling, Tracy flatly turned down the assignment. During this period, Tracy had a drinking problem and the studio executives treated him gently rather than bring on a crisis."

On May 16, Metro announced it had the next film property for Tracy, his first since winning the Oscar. He was to play Hernandez Coronado in a new historical epic by Dale Van Every and Tom Kilpatric. It was still in pre-production and far from ready for the cameras, and would be shot away from the studio in wilderness locations and deserts. Spencer used that information for leverage, saying he preferred going before the cameras immediately. He needed to work, thrived on his acting, and loved movies. He started demanding that he must work now. The studio heads countered by telling him they just happened to have one other highly suitable property available to meet his need. They offered Tracy the role of Father Flanagan once more.

To play a priest again, within a few years of *San Francisco*, and to portray a living personality, sent shock waves into Tracy. Always insecure, displaying a frightening inability to face new projects, he turned to alcohol, according to some accounts. The fear of playing the devout man could have been at the heart of Tracy's escape into alcoholic stupor.

Schary believed that Spencer Tracy's binge was "Homeric." It was rumored that he was found unconscious in his stable among his polo ponies. He required hospitalization, and Considine feared the film would have to be shelved.

For a while, the situation remained unclear. There were two diametrically different views on whether Tracy wanted to play Father Flanagan. A few thought the stress of playing a priest damaged his fragile psyche, and he could not face the failure in his own life to do something more important than acting. Others felt he considered the Flanagan role was a special honor, something he wanted to do as a testimonial to a great man, perhaps a spur to make him swear off drinking. What possibly sent him into an abyss of alcohol at this time may not have been the offer of Boys Town, but the earlier announcement that MGM planned to send him off to a wild location shoot for the film on the life of the Spanish conquistador. The *Coronado* property was shelved and never made into a film.

When Tracy recovered, the film about *Boys Town* was put on the fast track at Metro. Considine was prepared to move quickly before any other impediments stopped the production. Dore Schary later recalled, "I came to know Spence quite well. I learned about his quirks, especially his terrible insecurities about the pictures he did. Invariably he'd like a script and decide to do a picture; then he'd change his mind and say he absolutely wouldn't do it; and finally, usually just a few days before a film was ready to go, he'd reluctantly say, 'Okay, I'll do it.'"

According to Frank Sinatra who inquired of Tracy some years later, Spencer hated locations. The more far-flung and wild, the more he disliked it. Omaha may have looked rather civilized to Tracy, compared to re-enacting trips to the Grand Canyon. Later film projects, like *Northwest Passage*, soured him completely. Tracy disliked wearing make-up.

Father Flanagan's character guaranteed he could avoid that issue too. Another aspect, not often recognized, was the issue of working with children. Tracy expressed scorn for 'cute kid' actors. Though he thought Bartholomew was not too bad in *Captains Courageous*, other young actors had no appeal for him. The idea of a film cast of precocious children made him cringe, but the role of Father Flanagan required a mental discipline that challenged the actor. Plus the recent death of his friend, Will Rogers, who'd spoken to him during polo games of various charities he sponsored, created in Spence a desire to honor Rogers by filming a story of one of them—as he could with Boys Town.

Frank Whitbeck, a former Barnum and Bailey barker, born in 1882, was one of Howard Strickling's most important publicists at MGM. A tall, angular, bespectacled man with shiny silver hair, he was officially called an MGM executive, but he was most frequently a voice-over or narrator to many trailers or shorts. He did double-duty on the trip to Boys Town. He would serve as the narrator to *City of Little Men*, a Metro-Goldwyn-Mayer documentary about Boys Town that served as a warm-up to the film, and was produced simultaneously with the major motion picture.

Whitbeck's main function was to accompany the crew to Omaha was as watchdog over Tracy, to prevent any embarrassing episodes with alcohol and keep him out of trouble. Having the unusual hobby of keeping pet elephants from his circus days, he was strong and commanding enough to control Tracy. He traveled beside Tracy as company companion to public appearances, award dinners, and on location shoots. He went with Tracy in 1940 to Ripon College where the two-time Oscar winner received an honorary doctorate.

Mayer authorized Howard Strickling to handle problem stars like Spencer Tracy. For Tracy, Strickling later commented, "We devised an elaborate technique. We kept an official looking ambulance on call at the studio. Every bar owner and hotel manager in the area knew what to do if Tracy showed up drunk and began causing a problem. They'd phone me, and I'd phone Whitey (MGM Police Chief Hendry), and the ambulance would take off with a couple of our security men dressed as paramedics. They'd go to the scene, strap Tracy to a stretcher, and rush him away in the ambulance before too many people would recognize Tracy as the troublemaker."

Whitbeck was the main protector of Tracy from himself until 1941 when he met Katharine Hepburn. At that point and until the end of his career in 1967, she assumed the exhausting and sometimes thankless role of keeping him sober. As she noted, he could control himself during productions. In her tribute to Tracy decades later, she said: "Luckily he was able to overcome it for long periods of time. Not easy." He did seventy-four films, and most at MGM where people like Elizabeth Taylor, Robert Wagner, Lee Marvin, and Joan Bennett, sang his praises as the best film actor in the business.

MGM signed one of the foremost directors in Norman Taurog, known for his handling of child actors. Photo from author collection.

When May, 1938, approached, producer John Considine's difficulties seemed endless, though he had managed to weave the pre-production ingredients together. After the withdrawal of Jack Ruben from the picture for medical reasons, his first choice to direct, the producer was in a crisis.

Under pressure from Tracy, Considine brooked no delays. He knew of an available first-rate director, but not contracted to MGM. Norman Taurog directed one of the big hits of the year in *The Adventures of Tom Sawyer*, starring newcomer Tommy Kelly, a boy from the Bronx, who gave a startling performance in a movie, which remains a Technicolor marvel. Taurog's credentials beyond that were impeccable. Not well-remembered today, he won an early Oscar for

Skippy, a movie starring his nephew-in-law, Jackie Cooper. Taurog was known to elicit remarkable performances from children.

The *New York Times* of May 16, 1938, reported that Taurog had been inked by Metro for five years. Among the projects listed for him was the upcoming *Boys Town* with Spencer Tracy and Mickey Rooney. Press releases included Taurog as the future director of *The Wizard of Oz*, the plum of the year for most in the business. The *Oz* property may well have been the carrot dangled before Taurog to acquire his signature on the contract. MGM's announcement also stated that Father Flanagan had been invited to serve as Technical Adviser on the picture, a role he turned down.

In the years since his acme as a director, Taurog suffered a decline in his reputation after Jackie Cooper's notorious autobiography, the title of which was based upon an incident involving Taurog. *Please Don't Shoot My Dog* recounted the traumatic and cruel trick Taurog pulled on young Jackie during the making of *Skippy*. When the young actor would not cry, Taurog told a security guard to take the boy's little dog off the set and shoot it. Behind some curtains, Jackie heard the gunshot. He cried, and continued to do so for two days after everyone indicated it was a ruse to make him cry.

Whether spurious or not, the incident destroyed Taurog's reputation as one of the seminal 1930s directors. Described as roly-poly by kind observers, or "a fat Jew bastard" by his anti-Semite detractors, he was known during his salad days as a consummate director. Short, heavy-set, and quick-tempered, he often peered over his frameless glasses with displeasure. Cooper insisted his Uncle Norman screamed at children and threatened to replace Jackie because he was a "ham actor."

Norman Taurog was a studio-style director. He gave his producers a professional product, without delays, and always under budget. His later pictures included stars like the comedy team of Martin and Lewis as well as Elvis Presley, each of whom admired him and wanted him to direct more of their films.

A top-rated actor among a pantheon of male stars at MGM, Spencer Tracy was worth every ounce of care he required. He teamed well with other actors of like stature, such as Clark Gable, and the studio chose to pair Spence with one of their rising new Metro stars. Mickey Rooney was young, brash, with proven box-office potential, and conscious of his power.

From 1934 on the Metro lot, Mickey Rooney was blowing away the competition, especially fellow child performers like Jackie Cooper. It seemed Mickey got all the roles once given to Cooper; they were rivals, and intense about everything from music to girls. Signed at insistence of David O. Selznick, Rooney (called Mickey Maguire in an earlier incarnation as a small child star) was a fourteen-year-old dynamo and whirlwind. Like Shirley Temple, he was thought by some to be a midget. Said Rooney, "MGM always featured more juveniles than any other studio in Hollywood."

Mickey's infectious love of work was not an act. "You weren't going to work, you were going to have fun." Rooney absorbed L.B. Mayer's philosophy of studio life. "It was home, everybody was cohesive; it was family. One year I made nine pictures, I had to go from one set to another. It was like I was on a conveyer belt. You did not read a script and say I guess I'll do it. You did it. They had people that knew the kind of stories that were suited to you. It was a conveyer belt that made motion pictures."

Boys Town was just another film assignment in a busy year to Rooney in 1938. He never gave it much thought at the time. His bread and butter pictures were the Hardy series. It took a decade or more before he realized Whitey Marsh's lasting impact as a role. His tie to Boys Town grew in importance to him late in his career. At the time, Hollywood and movies were a lark.

Even in his earliest days in movies, Rooney studied aspects of the business. He often loitered around the electric, furniture, camera, and repair shops. His extroversion led him to be a leader and an instigator around the studios. Mickey organized baseball teams and football teams among the boys who worked with him in the comedies. Rough and tumble games were the ones Mickey liked to play behind the studio on the lawn. Rooney's days of wandering from studio to studio were over once he came to MGM, except for the occasional pictures when he was loaned to another studio. He was settled again in one place, given a star's dressing room and a private school teacher. Marching on the road to stardom, he was a featured player.

Mickey completed his grammar school and high school education in the small, one-story schoolhouse in the MGM studio, which has housed o many famous pupils. The little schoolhouse was a studio recreation of a one-room classic country school, but it was set in the shade of a huge concrete soundstage.

Presided over by Miss Mary McDonald, only the regular studio contract players attend the little school. Other teachers taught the extra children and the juvenile featured players who visited the studio for only one or two pictures, on the stage where they worked. There was a caste system worst than in the most segregated classrooms in the country at that time. During studio times MGM held regular classes three hours a day for the youngsters in the pictures. When the company worked outdoors, the tables and blackboards were set under a tree. When they worked inside the stage, a schoolroom was arranged in a quiet corner, away from the confusion and activity of the set. Usually there were two weeks of rest between the pictures.

Then, Mickey went back to public school and to his outside studio playmates. This disruption in continuity of Mickey's studies seemed to make no impact on adults, educators, or the studio. Child actors really lived two lives, one as the young star of the popular short comedies, the other as a normal kid, living an ordinary every day life.

During the shooting of *Boys Town*, Rooney gave the *New York Times* an interview in which he spoke about his hopes for the future. Like so many actors before and since, after he began to have successful in the MGM films, Mickey Rooney expressed an interest in becoming a movie director. "Mickey's employers around the MGM lot are doing everything, in a friendly way to thwart, or at least to defer, fulfillment of this latest desire. Their objections are not based so much on Mickey's age as on the fact that, as an actor who couldn't easily be replaced. Whether such a policy would prevail with the irrepressible Mr. Rooney remains to be seen."

According to the *Times*, Mickey's amazing antics and energy made him "one of the few players in pictures who makes the traditional white lies of press agent totally superfluous." If Mickey Rooney were spoiled, difficult, temperamental, or irresponsible, it seemed to come from his smash success. Everything he did made an impact in movies. He organized his own orchestra in the style of Benny Goodman and Paul Whiteman. He began to write popular songs and think of movies as a sidebar.

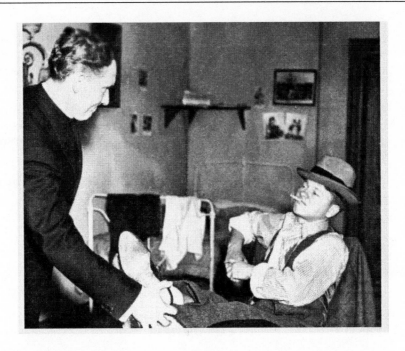

Mickey Rooney defies Spencer Tracy in one of the best-remembered scenes from Boys Town. Photo from the author's collection.

Not everything was rosy at Metro. Rooney caused Mayer plenty of trouble. Called into the inner sanctum of L.B.'s white office, the big man chastised him: "I've been hearing stories around town. I hear you've never met a pretty girl that you didn't kiss."

Rooney laughed it off, but Mayer was unrelenting. "I'm not talking about kissing." He made it clear he was talking about sexual liaisons, lots of them.

"Look, you like being Andy Hardy?"

Mickey said a limp, "Yes."

"Then be Andy Hardy."

Mickey claimed he stormed out of Mayer's office in a snit. Later, when the chief executive heard Rooney was involved with Norma Shearer, the widow of Irving Thalberg, Mayer went crazy: grabbing his star by the lapels. "You're Andy Hardy. You're the United States. You're a symbol. Behave yourself."

Long after the pinnacle of his career at Metro, Mickey realized much about his work during those days: "Mayer had his impossible moments, but he was, after all, the man who kept the store going. These were halcyon years." He made three Andy Hardy pictures right before *Boys Town*, and followed it up by playing Huck Finn. "I suppose deep underneath I knew that it couldn't last forever. I wouldn't be No. 1 at the box office or the world forever . . . How could I know about failure? I'd never failed at anything . . . I wasn't reliable . . . I didn't send Christmas cards or Christmas gifts. Mr. Mayer and I were friends in those days. It was on a very shallow level, but we were friends . . ."

Rooney believed that MGM was strictly a mirror of L.B.'s attitude. The stars had to live according to "Mr. Mayer's idea of morality. We were turning out mass entertainment, and we were turning it out fast."

Boys Town would prove to be one of the quickest edited and released of all MGM's movies. Mickey was a performer, but he was all business, highly professional. He was not social among all his co-workers. "We were actors, not buddies." He tended to ignore the advice of older or wiser heads. "Hell, when I was 18, I didn't have any troubles. I wanted no clues. I was the hottest young actor in Hollywood."

While making *Boys Town*, Mickey's status at the studio went sky-high with his box-office appeal. The public clamored for his next film, and the starring role in *Boys Town* was to be a top-level picture for him, one of his first as star. He was very proud when MGM gave him a star's dressing room, into which he moved in 1938. Before that time he dressed in one room in a long, two-story building which housed the featured players' quarters. Now he dressed in the "star building" with fellow actors, Clark Gable and Spencer Tracy, as his next-door neighbors.

Mickey commented: "Boy! I was surely was proud the day they moved me into my new dressing room. I know I'm only a kid, but it makes me feel grown up to be dressing in the same building with Clark and Spencer and the other men of the studio."

Rooney's new digs in the star wing included a paneled living room, furnished with deep easy chairs, a radio, low tables and a desk. The second room served as the real dressing room, with a man-sized mirror and a roomy closet to hold Mickey's clothes, as well as the wardrobe being used in his current motion picture.

Mickey's motto was: "If anything's worth doing at all, it's worth doing well." When he acted in a picture, according to a studio biography, he "thinks, dreams, talks that picture. During the making of a Hardy family film, he stops being Mickey Rooney and becomes Andy Hardy, at home as well as in the studio."

Rooney was playing the tough young city boy, whose heart was finally reached by Father Flanagan in *Boys Town*. The young actor tried to live like that youthful street Arab, always talking to cast and crew in that other boy's smart-aleck slang. Mickey's mother understood and encouraged him in his admiration for Spencer Tracy.

Mickey effused and displayed his usual sparkle of energy: "Gosh, if I could only be an actor like Spencer Tracy! The best part is that he's not only a swell actor, he's a swell guy too."

The test of their professionalism would be their location work on the new film about Father Flanagan.

5

ON LOCATION AT BOYS TOWN

On June 4th, John Considine approved the final changes. John Meehan added his editorial comments and corrections. His contribution to the film was to take the two diverse screen stories and join them together. First, the original Eleanor Griffin tale of the roots of the boys' home in 1917 remained as a prologue with its own boys and conflicts. Employing *montage* to depict the building of the campus, the story leaped ahead fifteen years to a second major storyline, this one featuring an incorrigible named Whitey Marsh.

This was the Schary contribution. To this merged script, John Meehan gave his approval and on June 13, 1938, was credited along with Dore Schary as screenwriter of the motion picture. MGM arranged for the crew and cast to take the train to Nebraska's Omaha Union Station from downtown Los Angeles. They departed on Friday night, June 24th, eager to eat their dinners on board. At capacity number of passengers on the train, the dining car was jammed; it took several hours to feed everyone. The two-day jaunt lasted until Sunday afternoon, June 26th, in the state's capitol.

Before the company left for Boys Town, the Screen Actors Guild had taken an interest in the production plans to hire extras on location. An item in the *New York Times* stated: "The studios have an agreement with the Guild under which non-members may be used in pictures beyond a 300-mile radius form Hollywood. Fearing that the producers will take advantage of this leeway, according to Pat Somerset, in most cases the Guild sends a representative in advance of the troupe to advise the local people of their rights and of standard pay and working conditions. Generally the non-professional extras are glad to get Guild scale, although no attempt is made by the organization to force the issue."

By the time the cast and crew arrived at Omaha, representatives of SAG had preceded the crew and apprised Father Flanagan of the rights of the boys and how much they'd be paid for appearing as extras in the film. Sizeable amounts of money were involved because the studio used over a hundred boys as extras for each day, providing Boys Town with a hefty payment.

The 1600 mile ride from Los Angeles to Albuquerque, on to Kansas City, and then to Lincoln, had multiple stops before the final, short ride northeastward to Omaha. The trip was an opportunity to acquaint the cast and their crew. Though the stars kept their usual aloofness staying in private cabins while others bunked in sleeping cars, everyone mingled socially at meals in the dining car and in the passenger carriages.

For Gene Reynolds, at fifteen an up-and-coming Metro contract player with featured billing, this was a major location trip without his mother along. It was a passage toward adulthood. Said Gene, "I was fifteen and my mother did not go with me." He found it luxurious and a thrill. "The train ride was very nice, a lot of fun. We had bunks."

Enjoying the upper and lower berths, the half-dozen juveniles were off on an adventure. Because of school issues, the entire production was conveniently planned to coincide at the end of classes for the juveniles. One of them had a final school task uncompleted. Frankie Thomas, fresh from his leading role in *Tim Tyler's Luck*, a Saturday matinee serial for Universal studios, had been cast in MGM's film for a minor role as the mayor of Boys Town. He said: "I actually graduated from Hollywood High on a train to Omaha. I was not able to attend my graduation. My mother went down to the principal and said I should still receive my diploma. She told them I was off to Nebraska. When they announced the commencement list at the high school during the ceremony, I wasn't there. So it was specially awarded to me during our trip to the location."

By that, he no doubt meant they had announced his graduation along with the rest of the seniors, but turned over the diploma to his mother.

Including multiple stops along the way, there were short periods of time for the boys and others to de-train and stretch their legs. Feeling quite responsible, Gene chose to follow many others who left the train, "We had a twenty-minute stopover in Kansas City and I got off the train. The tracks led up to a lobby through a stairwell, but there were many identical doors. After a few minutes, I couldn't recall which door led back to the train. I was so scared." He frantically looked for the right exit to his train. "After a few minutes of running around in a panic I saw some of our crew and followed them back to the train."

During the journey the most social man on the train was Norman Taurog. As a last minute hire to direct this film, he hadn't a chance to visit Boys Town. Jack Ruben had scouted the locations he expected to use. Taurog relied on second-hand reports. As a new hire at Metro, the director used the leisurely train ride to build relationships among cast and crew.

Norman Taurog, as everyone knew, worked well with children. Though not in the caliber of Clarence Brown, whom Gene Reynolds had just finished *Of Human Hearts*, the director was respected among the juvenile actors. He personally picked the boys for the film in consultation with John Considine.

An A-film director, he knew well the work of Hollywood's regular performers. Hiring someone close to the leading actors was often a concession made to stars. Mickey Rooney, becoming powerful with each picture in 1938, requested his own personal companion and stand-in, Dick Paxton. Mickey also enjoyed spending time with Sid Miller, another actor chosen for the youthful cast. Both went along for the shoot.

Back then, Frankie Thomas insisted, "casting directors used to be less important. They were just gophers." On this production Taurog told agents and studio which youngsters would best work under his highly efficient system; eight boys were on the train: Mickey, of course, and Gene Reynolds, Sid Miller, Bobs Watson, Frankie Thomas, and Jimmy Butler. Two other boys made the trip, but one was later dismissed from the picture while on location.

Everyone spoke highly of young Butler whose career might have been a glorious one in Hollywood, except for heroic tragedy. A volunteer for military service, Jimmy Butler was to die in uniform while in France, fighting in the war only a few years later. He was beloved by cast members and soon to be missed.

Taurog selected performers who gave him what he expected. He planned for less trouble on the set, with fewer takes because of seasoned

WILLIAM RUSSO & JAN MERLIN

actors. The smoother it went for the director, the more relaxed he'd be during the shoot. Frankie recalled, "Taurog left us alone to do the job. There were a few directors like that."

During that long ride, Taurog reserved a dinner table for two late in the evening in order to speak with Frankie. While they ate, he discussed the philosophy of playing a character role as the seventeen-year old mayor. Norman found the blond lad shyer than most child actors, and wanted to learn more about him.

Frankie had the difficult role of playing foil to Mickey Rooney, who had the best lines, chewed scenery, and knew all the tricks of keeping audience eyes on himself. Taurog made sure Frankie knew how to work with such a character. Frankie recalled: "I thought it was pretty easy to play off Mickey. Everything he did made me look good. And it was mutual. It was my job to make the leading man look better."

The son of professional actors, Frankie hardly needed tutelage. He knew what to do and how to do it. What emerged from his conversation with Norman likely comforted the director. Frankie required little coaching or coaxing from his director, which removed the burden of worry about one young cast member. Instruction was clear. "You always know when some character actor is making you look good," commented Frankie.

Taurog also avoided one of the inevitable activities among traveling Hollywood crews: the great on-going poker game. It went on all night and continued throughout the following day. Not a participant, Frankie noted, "A lot of money was on the table. I was playing a bit of bridge back then, but nothing like this. You had stand-ins and the guys who couldn't afford to lose. They were out betting the most. The grips, the cameramen."

There were sixty-one people, combined cast and crew, from MGM on the train, with sub-cultures and cliques that remained steadfast. Everyone in the Metro family knew his place, and seldom tried to move into another group.

When they arrived on late afternoon of June 26, 1938, what seemed like the entire state of Nebraska was assembled at the train station to welcome the cast and crew of the *Boys Town* film. They'd be at the village for a planned ten days of location shooting. For Nebraskans, movie magic dropped into their laps, never to be forgotten. The new visitors were shocked and pleased to see so many thousands greeting them at Omaha's Union Station.

58

Impressed by the welcome, Frankie said, "Everyone was at the train station, and as we drove through the city to our hotel, the streets were deserted." The warmth of the welcome of Omaha's community seemed to entail everyone who lived there.

Talent accommodations were booked at the Hotel Fontenelle. Tracy, Taurog, and Rooney, had suites to themselves. The featured and lesser players shared rooms. Bobs Watson, who was in the custody of his father Coy, stayed with him. Frankie said he shared a suite of two bedrooms and a sitting room with other young actors. "We had two beds in two rooms. Nice hotel, nothing really distinctive." Crew also doubled up in their rooms. "We had a big suite. One of the guys was out every night and he was always borrowing my sports coats."

When Frankie went to breakfast at the hotel dining room the next morning, he noticed, "There were girls around the elevator. Young girls. Soon they were on the same floor around the elevator. They wanted to be invited in, but we were very careful. They weren't chasing me for my autograph."

Though they were on a tight schedule, the crew had to go out to Boys Town on the first day to set up. It left the young actors free for a while. When Gene Reynolds met Father Flanagan, there was an instant rapport. The priest was pleased to see the actor who would portray the crippled boy. "He took an interest in me," recalled Gene. To him, like so many others, the demure and self-effacing priest was "very nice."

The first duty of the troupe was a big gathering at one of the local theaters that night. It was meant as an opportunity to introduce everyone to the city of Omaha and to the village of Boys Town. Father Flanagan was also to be on the stage during the assembly.

The Omaha Theatre itself was packed, every seat at a premium. Many invited guests and dignitaries of the community welcomed the Hollywood troupe, and a few seats remained open to the general public. Thomas recollected the procedure of the greeting. "Everyone was introduced by someone else. Mick was introduced. They were trying to get the cooperation of the local residents."

Through some system he'd forgotten Frankie Thomas found himself with the honor of introducing Father Flanagan who would in turn introduce Spencer Tracy, and so on down the line. Mickey Rooney was the last one to jump up on stage and wave to the ecstatic crowd. Frankie was unfazed by the staged ceremony.

"Oh, we used a sliding scale to decide who would introduce Father Flanagan. One of the actors in the picture introduced someone else and they introduced me and then I gave the intro to Father Flanagan."

Before they went out on stage, Frankie asked the founder of Boys Town, "Is there anything you want me to mention, Father?"

He knew Frankie was to play the Mayor of Boys Town, and he was deferential. "Say, whatever you think is important." Frankie thought he was quite professional, so composed. "You would have thought he was an actor." And, the young actor believed this quality came from the priest's constant need to go before the public and present himself and his community.

Gene Reynolds did not recall attending what Frankie Thomas so clearly described. Upon reflection so many decades after the occasion, Frankie noted: "I thought Father Flanagan was perfect as a small town Midwestern priest, and here he was looking like the complete opposite of a man who was running a major operation. To be the motivating factor in a unique situation, I would never have thought it in a million years."

Bobs Watson who played Pee Wee related his first sight of Father Flanagan during one of his return visits to Boys Town many years later to attend a dedication. He told of the morning he was in Boys Town for the first time: "I saw this beautiful man, tall. I had to look way up to him. And the day that I first saw him he was wearing one of those straw hats because it was so blooming hot here. He looked down to me, and I was introduced to him." Gene confirmed the unbearable heat of the Nebraska summer, which was an initial shock to his system. "It was hot as the Dickens there. I wasn't used to it, being from California. The humidity surprised me."

All the Hollywood witnesses were mainly in agreement. Mickey Rooney spent a great deal of time with the founder of Boys Town while they were in Omaha and said: "Father Flanagan is one of the grandest men I have ever met." The priest was quite tall and thin, soft-spoken. Yet, his voice had carrying power.

Frankie said that when Father Flanagan stepped on stage to bring out Spencer Tracy, "He talked about how these performers had come all the way from Hollywood to help bring Boys Town to more people and more countries. The people there loved it. Here, I thought, is a gentleman who has led Boys Town. I recall he was on his home base there in Omaha. I believe he always tried to say something nice about people."

Cast members Frankie Thomas, Mickey Rooney, Sid Miller, Bobs Watson, and Gene Reynolds, on location in Boys Town. Photo courtesy of Frankie Thomas.

The next morning the film crew was ready to start. A fleet of Omaha cabs was assigned to take cast and crew about ten miles out to Boys Town every morning with a police escort getting them through streets that were not deserted. Those cabs were on call all day. If anyone had to leave Boys Town, they weren't running on the meter.

Gene Reynolds, eventually to play one of the fictional mayors, thought the drive from Omaha quiet, lacking roadside activity or buildings, and he admired the "miles of prairie and farm land." He found the Boys Town village to be spacious; its main building, post office, gymnasium, centered on a quadrangle, "the square where we filmed." Many scenes, too, took place on a "long roadway leading from the main gate."

The other fictional mayor, Frankie Thomas, stated: "We came out every morning, fairly early. We'd start shooting around 9. We shot all day, and this was summer. It was very warm in the afternoons. I figured no one would be there early in the morning. Oh, man, they were there to see us. It was a mammoth crowd."

Since Boys Town was an open campus, the public was able to travel the extra miles to see their favorite stars at work. Police details were also needed for security, though Gene Reynolds reported the crowds were unobtrusive. Gene thought the number of spectators was small each day, which led him to conclude they were on a closed set.

Displaying natural exuberance and extroversion, Mickey Rooney was hard to hold down. After signing autographs for many adoring girls, Mickey was still hyperactive. Frankie didn't like to play sports while working on a film and may have been concerned about injuring himself during a shoot. His natural caution bore no resemblance to Mickey's attitude. "I turned around once he was out there playing football with these kids. I know why he was doing it. He wanted to show he was one of the boys. Taurog must have had an ulcer. Supposing he slipped or hurt himself? But there was no holding him!"

As far as the featured cast was concerned, they came to Boys Town to do their job, and they did the work as efficiently as possible. In one response about the location filming, Boys Town's Thomas J. Lynch, resident historian, agreed that Spencer Tracy and Mickey Rooney were guests of Father Flanagan "on numerous occasions."

Frankie Thomas heard of a tour of hospitality for the director and major stars conducted by officials at Boys Town. He believed, for the most part, Father Flanagan was busy with his administrative duties.

Many of the location scenes occurred outside of Father Flanagan's office; he witnessed the daily activities from his window. For one scene, Spencer Tracy entered and exited the front door of the very building where the Father had his office. At least once per day the priest tried to make a visit to wherever the company was shooting.

However much Father Flanagan was around, he never offered any suggestions for scenes. He allowed the professionals from Hollywood to do their work without interruption, seldom speaking with Taurog. Frankie observed that a still photographer was in attendance with Father Flanagan wherever he went, but was never sure if the photographer worked for Metro or Boys Town.

"We never toured the place," answered another cast member. "It probably never occurred to them to give us (the supporting cast) a tour. But it was very spacious. I thought the buildings were far apart." Since one of Frankie's first tasks in the film was to conduct a tour of the facility for the arrogant Whitey Marsh, it was also the first time he'd seen what he was pointing out to Mickey, the other actor.

Frankie did make a special trip to see "the agricultural fields where many of the boys worked. It was impressive and big. It amazed me how Father Flanagan knew how to get the money to build it." Gene recalled hearing a conversation Father Flanagan had with a few of the notables on the film. There was suggestive mention of how "women came out of the woodwork in Omaha with lots of fraternizing."

While Reynolds remained standing quietly on the periphery of the cast, Father Flanagan pointed at him and said to the others, "There's a boy who will never be corrupted."

Spencer Tracy, a loner and highly private person, was alternately warm and wonderful, or cold and hard to get to know. He once scoffed at a reporter who asked him about his private life. After delivering a withering Tracy glare, he shot back. "Now you're kidding me. There is no such thing as a private life in this town."

A curmudgeon, Tracy's personality led to many extremes in the reactions of those who met him. "Oh, to me he was wonderful to work with." Said Frankie Thomas, "He was professional, and he was removed unless he knew you or knew something on you."

Frankie was a clever lad who'd spent his entire childhood and adolescence among adults, so he was shrewd when it came to the best approach to reach the aloof Mr. Tracy. At an opportune moment, he 'accidently' bumped into the star as he came off filming a scene in his full priestly regalia. "I said, 'Mr. Tracy, you're still a member of the Lambs, aren't you?'"

This was totally unexpected. Who would expect film actors to know about Edwin Booth's most prestigious and exclusive club in the business? And from a teenage boy, of all people in Omaha, asking him about the New York's oldest legitimate theatrical club? Spencer Tracy never invited conversation, and was caught off-guard. The cherubic blond actor said, "Do you remember Frank M. Thomas?"

Once again Tracy was taken aback. He inquired with wary surprise. "How do you know about that club and Frank?"

The boy playing Freddie Fuller separated himself from the crowd. "I told him I was Frank's son." Being the son of professional actors gave young Frankie a kind of royal pedigree in the business. "My father and uncle knew him quite well." Though neither his father, nor uncle, worked with Tracy on Broadway, they were long-time acquaintances at the Lambs. Stage actors coming to the West Coast after 1930 formed a snobbish camaraderie when facing a generation of film-based actors populating the industry. Tracy was delighted. "You're Frank's boy. Well, for Heaven's sake."

After that introduction, he was extremely pleasant to Frankie.

Mickey Rooney's acrobatics do not impress Frankie Thomas. Standing by are Sid Miller and Bobs Watson. Photo courtesy of Frankie Thomas.

Since Father Flanagan was around the set and Frank Whitbeck near at hand, Tracy behaved himself. Although the Oscar-winner could blow a line, or misspoke a word, he'd say, "Sorry, kids." They'd do a retake, but that was rare. "The kids in *Boys Town* never broke up much. If one goes, they'd all go. We would not dare look at each other. The children-actors never did that while making *Boys Town*."

Questioned regarding any egotistic performance, Frankie said: "I don't recall Tracy fussing about the lighting or anything like that. All the crew knew what they must do to make the picture a success."

Tracy trusted in the professionals that MGM put on his crew to make these pictures the best they could be.

Nor was Tracy uncomfortable playing an American icon so beloved by the country. In that way, Tracy's personality gave him an advantage. Flanagan had a good choice suggesting Tracy to play the role. There was really no one else who could do it. Frankie held firm in his view: "But I think Father Flanagan got him that Academy Award. When I see the picture again, I really think the film was meant to salvage the youth of America and that likely got him the award."

Though MGM wanted a technical advisor for Tracy to play a priest, and they had offered the off-screen job to Father Flanagan, there really was no need for that. Tracy had a few conversations with the cleric and quickly assimilated what technical information he needed.

Roman Catholic, if a bit lapsed, Tracy still knew enough about the priesthood to perform the role as designated in the script. Once back at Metro, higher-ups would have another opinion. Tracy had heard much about Father Flanagan from his old pal, Will Rogers, a long-time friend and supporter of the priest and his humanitarian endeavors, dating back to the mid-1920s.

During his encounters and conversations, Tracy studied Flanagan for clues to play him on screen. At their first dinner together, the actor learned much about Boys Town and the thoughtful and constructive approach, which Father Flanagan employed to help boys with problems.

Whatever acting 'tricks' Tracy pulled from his bag, he discarded them for this movie. Spencer attempted to play a modest but open man, "without mannerisms or idiosyncrasies, devout but not sanctimonious, a man of great physical as well as emotional strength. And he was attractive, extremely masculine."

Biographer Larry Swindell concluded Tracy simply decided he must pattern his performance on reality. He did ignore one detail. Spencer preferred not to wear the straw hat that was one of Father Flanagan's trademarks. Nonetheless, the star worked hard at presenting the dignity and strength of Father Flanagan in quiet and intense gestures.

As evidence of how dedicated to the role he became, upon meeting the special boy-police force of the Town, he devised a surprise gift for them. He immediately ordered a rush creation of genuine police badges, at his own expense. He was delighted to be able to deliver them before he finished the location work.

Having designed the badges himself and, in the days before priority and rush shipping, the gifts were ready for presentation on the Sunday before the Fourth of July. Filming that day, and in costume as Father Flanagan, he personally pinned the chief's badge on Patrick McKenna in a ceremony recorded by photographers. It was noted that none of Spencer's scenes had need for a technical advisor, though one was listed on the manifest during filming.

Spencer's performance was based on his own knowledge of the faith that sustained him through so many dark and desperate times. "What scene required him to use a technical advisor?" asked Frankie Thomas. "He could have been on the set, but there is quite a lot I have not seen. I can't say an MGM priest wasn't there, but I simply never saw him." Whether Frankie realized it or not, Father Flanagan was Spencer Tracy's technical advisor and role model, all in one.

Spencer Tracy donated badges to the Boys Town police, run by the residents, and pinned the Chief of Police between takes on location. Photo courtesy of the Omaha World Tribune.

6

BEHIND THE SCENES
AT BOYS TOWN

Mickey Rooney exploded onto the nation's psyche with his Andy Hardy movies, but the performance in *Boys Town* solidified his drawing power. MGM decided to put a rush on the production after seeing the growing interest in their rising new star. Previously in supporting and smaller roles, he was placed on equal footing with the Oscar winner, Spencer Tracy. Metro began to see how this team of Tracy and Rooney could render them huge box-office benefits. The picture hurried toward completion.

Over two years ago at Metro, Mickey had observed Tracy. While playing a small supporting role in *Captains Courageous*, Rooney had learned enough to try to match the Oscar winner in their *Boys Town* scenes.

Frankie Thomas remarked it would never occur to Tracy see Mickey as a competitor. "Mickey did not steal the movie. Yes, he was colorful. I am certain he (Tracy) never expected Mickey to steal the picture. Tracy was too egotistical to think this pint-sized actor could run off with the movie, and up to that time Mickey had played only featured roles. He had been active, but suddenly became big."

Others knew Mickey could turn serious when he wished to focus his performance. Something in the Flanagan story of the disadvantaged boys seemed to touch Rooney. "I think *Boys Town* is a wonderful place," said the star years later in one of his autobiographies. He was interested in the boys and liked chatting with them. "Between scenes we'd sit around and talk. I made a lot of good friends there and I hope see all of them again." He would, indeed, years later. He can still be caught wearing a sweatshirt with BOYS TOWN imprinted on the front.

Mickey was always raring to go to work. He explained during an interview in 2005 how *Boys Town* represented quick and professional work. He recalled the actual length of shooting in Omaha was a mere six days. "And we spent six days at the studio shooting," though he referred to his own scenes, not the entire picture's daily work.

Decades later, the picture was something special for Rooney. He never tired of talking about it, and was greatly proud of his work in it. The role of Whitey Marsh was vigorous and lively, every scene was exciting to play and every line of dialogue crackled. The star would say in the morning, "On-time Rooney, that's me. Where do we start this morning?"

From Rooney's perspective, he was only doing his job, and doing it well. "Movies like books and plays attempt to create an illusion of reality." Mickey did not mix his movie roles with his life. Doing this job professionally, he'd only become bigger and bigger. The part of Whitey catapulted his high salary to astronomical 1938 levels, as much as $5000 per week.

When Mickey Rooney was on the set, not one of his peers tried to top him. Mickey was always on, always performing. The stereotype of the hyperactive dynamo was about as accurate as any in Hollywood. He was forever doing vaudeville *schtick* when he wasn't actually on set for filming. His routines were a constant barrage of jokes. He was overwhelming and sucked the air out of every room he entered. Gene Reynolds noted, "Some of us would make a witty remark now and then, but Mickey was always on."

Watching this little titan was amazing for young Gene. He started to marvel at him while on the Andy Hardy movie they had done earlier, in the year when Gene took on a recurring part in what would become a decade-long series as Jimmy McMahon. "You know he never read a script. He couldn't sit still long enough to read one. I bet he never read a script through to the end in his entire life."

The value and importance of Sid Miller in many of Mickey's movies was evident on *Boys Town*. "He'd have Sid read him the plot every day. I can recall Miller explaining a scene and how it ended."

Sid would consult the script and told Mickey, "You do this and this . . ."

Mick responded, "Then what?"

Miller told him, "And then you do that . . ."

Rooney answered, "No kidding?" He had no idea of the plot. When the young star reached the end of a sequence, Sid revealed what happened in the script. Mickey would say, "Why that little son of a bitch!" Then, the irrepressible Mickey would go out and do it for the camera.

In that era, movies were made at a far slower pace than is done today. Since barely three pages of script would be filmed in a day, Mickey came in each morning, looked over his lines of dialogue, read them once, and tossed the pages aside. He had them memorized. In the business, he was known as "a quick study."

Acting up was second nature to him. Like Tracy, Rooney was a problem for Mayer and the studio. His judgment was not always level headed, but it was clearly the result of a huge talent, a sense of his own importance, and a need to achieve, driven perhaps by the inadequacies he felt about his height. The studio was happy to place on payroll one of the new entourage for Mickey. His best friend was, in fact, like Frank Whitbeck for Tracy, a kind of keeper. Mickey found his own keeper at a roller skating rink.

Before long, he was Rooney's closest friend, going so far as to move into the Rooney household. They were the same size and age, and so Dick Paxton took on the role of Mickey's stand-in. He also made sure Mickey did not lose too much at the track, didn't smoke in public, and maintained a cover for the frequent and various dates Mickey made with the 'ladies.' Paxton was mature and understood his role as Mickey's constant companion. Everywhere Mickey went, Paxton followed.

Becoming a friend to Mickey after they'd met on the train to Omaha (what fellow young actor wasn't charmed and taken in by Mickey?), Frankie Thomas actually found the sedate and quiet Paxton more akin to his own interests. "I knew Dick quite well," commented Frankie. "Mickey and Dick did not look at all alike. Dick used to act like a chauffeur. He'd go out, pick up, and deliver all of Mickey's dates. Mickey didn't spend his time driving around town."

Frankie's own stand-in usually was a man old enough to be his father, and one assigned by the studio. While in Omaha, Frankie and Dick had a chance to become better acquainted, as Dick was assigned to share the suite at Hotel Fontenelle with Frankie, while Mickey had a suite to himself down the hall. Frankie remembered mostly, "Paxton was one of the few people I ever saw who could do a one-armed pull-up. Amazing! He was very athletic. Tennis, golf, swimming, you name it—and always with Mickey."

The other member of Mickey's entourage was Sid Miller who played Mo Kahn in the cast. Sid and Mickey had been writing songs together, appearing in the same musicals, and frequently Sid served as Master of Ceremonies at nearly all of Mickey's Hollywood parties.

Publicity photo of Tracy as Father Flanagan and Rooney as Whitey Marsh. Photo from author's collection.

Of the six actors cast to play *Boys Town* juveniles, Sid was the oldest to play one of the resident boys. At twenty-two, he was portraying the Jewish barber role, and had done five to ten pictures per year all through the 1930s. Bobs Watson, at seven during filming, was the veteran of a dozen pictures and the youngest.

In between in age was Gene Reynolds, (fifteen-years old with an equal number of pictures), billed with Henry Hull and Leslie Fenton under the film title as co-stars, Jimmy Butler (seventeen, and playing the older bus driver), Frankie Thomas (seven months younger than Rooney), and of course, Mickey (who was a major star at seventeen).

Frankie appeared to be tallest of the juvenile players, and says ruefully that fact had the year before lost him the lead role of Andy Hardy when it was given to Mickey Rooney. One problem with all young performers was their competition. Many believed Mickey had displaced Jackie Cooper and driven him out of Metro and into the Poverty Row studio, Monogram.

Freddie Bartholomew had taken roles away from Frankie, and Gene Reynolds was receiving a Metro build-up, which meant he would finally take roles that might have gone to Frankie, had he been put under contract.

"When Gene came on, he was quite small, but he was around the same age as I was," came the assessment from the chagrined actor. "Now what experience he had to justify his winning the part, I don't know." It may have been sour grapes on Frankie's part. Gene Reynolds enjoyed co-star billing and a contract for five years at MGM.

Gene's roommate/actor in Omaha at the Fontenelle was also a buddy with an Irish look and a devoted Catholic. After some cajoling, the roommate dragged a reluctant Gene to Mass in Omaha, but he felt awkward since he was Jewish. During the service, the priest in his sermon made a remark about Jews taking over the church if donations were not maintained. Gene knew he'd made the wrong decision to attend that Sunday morning.

One night Gene's roommate arranged a double date with a couple of local girls. They went to a movie and had sodas at a local malt shop. One girl's brother was chaperone and driver of their car. He carelessly took his eyes off the road for a moment, and they suffered a car crash, Gene wound up hobbling, but his friend severely hurt his ankle when his foot went under the front seat.

Though Gene didn't think this was a bad accident, the hullabaloo was dramatic when he returned to the hotel. The hue and cry of the Metro people made him decide not to tell his mother about this incident on his first adult trip. To Gene's dismay, his roommate on picture was fired! Taurog or another MGM executive on the location carried out the dismissal.

No one there 'recalled' that boy's name decades later. Somewhat older than Gene Reynolds, and liked by the young rising Metro star, the roommate was meant to be a stable influence and protector of his charge. By involving the film's fifth billed star in an accident, this young actor failed his responsibility. His time on screen in *Boys Town* was negligible and the next year, in perhaps a makeup for the firing, Norman Taurog gave the boy a small role, playing a bellhop in a crowded hotel scene in a forgettable picture. It coincided with the end of the bit player's movie career.

Gene, an MGM contract star and a key player in the film, was in his mid-teens. The other boy was mainly there to be a watchful, older companion. It was an arrangement made secretly by the MGM management. The reputation of their stars was paramount, and everything unpleasant was to be kept from the newspapers. Gene's car accident was another studio secret.

What the film did for these performers was make clear what the future held. Gene Reynolds said much later, "I thought Mickey was really the big time." In Omaha, Mickey was light years ahead of the others. His prowess with girls and women impressed all the adolescents surrounding him. "He (Mickey) had humor, and humor is a great seducer. I think he would just laugh them into bed, and he had this incredible energy and gift for comedy."

Gene recalled one day after returning from the location at Boys Town. "Mickey said to me, 'You getting laid?' I was a wide-eyed fifteen-year old kid, and I said, 'no,' like a little kid that had never seen a circus. And Mickey kind of smiled and said, 'Well, everybody else is.'"

Frankie Thomas added later, "No, Gene wasn't alone."

The youngest member of the MGM players was Bobs Watson. Forever typecast as Pee Wee, the film and working on it had a tremendous impact on Bobs. The Watson brothers all worked in movies under the auspices of their father, Coy. Though most children had the proverbial 'stage mother,' the Watson boys had a 'stage father.' He traveled with Bobs to Boys Town and, depending on the witness, directed Bobs specifically in all his roles.

Bobs always expressed his deep gratitude to his father and had great respect for his assistance. Others felt less kind about the *pater familias* of one of Hollywood's biggest child star assembly line. Coy's six sons stood firmly behind the reputation of their father.

Gene Reynolds had worked with two of the brothers, including Bobs, a year earlier in the classic *In Old Chicago*, playing the O'Leary brothers as children in a Hollywood *homage* to the Great Chicago Fire. At that time Reynolds was a little shaken by the fact that Coy Watson had his boys crying full blast in rehearsals. Since Reynolds had a difficult time with the crying scenes, his confidence went flat at this sight. He'd never seen anything quite like it.

Gene related, "Coy Watson would go on job interviews with the boys." He offered them advice, and he controlled their careers. When a Watson boy grew too old for film roles, there was another younger one in the pipeline to take his place. Coy Watson ran a full-time business with his sons as actors. Once Gene ran up to the Watson boys' room in their hotel to see them when they arrived at a location.

To his surprise, they had not yet unpacked their bags, but Coy Watson had them rehearsing scenes and having them cry on the spot. Just with a look directly into their faces, the boys started to cry one by one.

So far as Gene was concerned, "Bobs was a good actor. He was a very talented and intelligent actor, as well as a very sweet man." Coy, his father once told Gloria Swanson, "Bobs is a good kid, and I guess he has a knack for screen acting."

As boys, the Watson brothers were all professional criers. To make himself better at the important act of crying on cue, Gene practiced while walking home each day from Bancroft Junior High School. He used all kinds of imaginative tricks to force tears from his eyes. During his early tries, it took him half a mile to bring tears. Then he made himself cry half way home on his walk. Finally, he was able to turn on the waterworks in one block with his intense concentration.

Though Frankie Thomas paid little attention to stage parents, his own were Broadway actors who began a career in Hollywood after he was 'discovered' and brought to the screen, he remembered and disputed strongly one of Bobs Watson's memories. Years after Tracy's death, Bobs insisted that he called Tracy "Uncle Spence," at the actor's request.

Frankie said flatly: "I can't see that. 'Uncle Spence?' Ohhh, what the hell was Bobs passing around here? Uh-uh. Of course, we all called him 'Mr. Tracy'. I would give you 100 to 1, not ten to one, that was not real. I did not know Tracy socially, but he was very pleasant on the set. If Spencer Tracy ran into Bobs a month later, he'd probably not recognize him."

Asked about the 'Uncle Spence' anecdote that Bobs circulated late in his career, Gene thought it was entirely possible. "I just don't know how close Tracy and Bobs were, but Bobs was a cute little guy."

Many had only the kindest words for Norman Taurog who oversaw these antics. In addition to directing the film, Taurog had his eye peeled for new talent. Hollywood studios were in a fad of allowing moppets to rule the screen; the director was cognizant how the next star could be the cute kid standing in the background. Rooney was always quick to cite Taurog as a "great director" sixty years after the picture was completed. For him Taurog epitomized the classic old style director who sat next to his camera, knew the set-ups, and worked efficiently. "Don't get me started," when it came to comparing the old directors with today's new breed.

To select extras, Taurog patiently listened to many of the boys living at the Town. If they played a harmonica, or could dance, he'd sit down and intently watch for that intangible quality that the camera might love. Thomas Lynch, the Historian of Girls and Boys Town, also noted that Taurog "had many interactions with the boys." Many photographs at the official Hall of History indicated this.

Taurog made some early films of merit, like Skippy. Later his work became mundane, ending his career with Elvis pictures. Films like *Boys Town* were good films, according to present-day producer Gene Reynolds who found his director "competent and energetic." They were not pictures of merit on the level of John Ford or Clarence Brown, whom Reynolds saw as artists of the first order. Taurog had a regular assistant whose job was to give him creative responses. This position was known in the industry as "a gag man." More accurately named, the job was Technical Director.

For Norman, the role was played by one of his constant associates for movies, Jack Mintz. Sometimes Mintz was called a dialogue coach, or assistant in some other capacity in all his decades of work at MGM. He'd been in movies all his adult life, truly active from the 1930s and kept his ties to Taurog. According to Gene Reynolds, Mintz would inform the director "if a scene was okay, if it needed this, if it needed that, kind of a creative influence." Mintz fulfilled the role that Clarence Brown or John Ford never required; their own instincts were acute enough.

Norman Taurog knew Mintz's brother, Sam, who wrote many screenplays, including a few at Paramount where Norman made his reputation directing Jackie Coogan and Junior Durkin in *Huckleberry Finn* while Sam wrote the prequel *Tom Sawyer* with the same cast. Sam was Jack's younger brother, a couple of Boston boys who came west in the early days of the studio relocation. Their ties to Taurog would last a lifetime.

Gene Reynolds, in later years, would later turn to production himself and saw that MGM was "was dominated by creative people in the Production Department. They had an obsession to efficiently get the movie in on time." Their power extended to how everything in a movie might be done. If weather was to impede progress, they switched the Call Sheet at the last minute to do a scene suitable to the meteorology.

In terms of weather, June was not a bad time to film outdoors in Nebraska. It was hot, but not terribly uncomfortable. Taurog had the luck to be out filming each day without any delays, including Saturday. They ran ahead of schedule. Taurog also had the fortune to have one-take shots for the most part.

Film footage was sent back to the studio by airplane each evening. It was returned the next day for Taurog to view. If there was anything he didn't like about it, he was able to shoot the scene again while at Boys Town. By keeping ahead of schedule, he kept a cushion for retakes. Whatever the conditions on the location, Taurog basically left the actors alone. Having selected them for their experience and talent, he trusted them to rely on their craft. Frankie Thomas insisted, "We worked all those weeks and he never said boo to me."

Normally directing like a man dressed for a dinner date in Beverly Hills, Taurog gave the public what was presumed the image of a Hollywood director on location. Like Alfred Hitchcock, Taurog usually wore fine suits and silk ties, but at Boys Town he paraded around in a pith helmet and safari jacket. Frankie Thomas speculated that it was likely worn for 'publicity fun.' Thomas acknowledged that some directors, particularly at Universal, "did the whole Cecil B. DeMille bit—jodhpurs and the like."

To control more than a hundred active and energetic non-actors who worked as extras was no easy task. As one of the resident boys who worked on the picture, Tom McGuire said during a reunion of the

Town boys, "Getting the crowd to calm down and follow the instructions: that was the most difficult as a group, getting us to calm down and follow the instructions. You know how kids are. We were no different."

Taurog used Jimmy Butler for this purpose. Though he was not much older than Mickey, he gave off an authoritative air and was mature beyond his years. Having several scenes as bus driver and aide to Father Flanagan in the movie, he also worked as an ersatz Assistant Director, serving as the boy wrangler. He kept them all in line. His "job was to solidify the kids. Jimmy Butler did that work expertly," said Frankie Thomas.

Not many on the crew suspected the hard lives and trouble some of the resident boys may have endured. On the location set, they were well behaved by the standards of the film professionals.

Gene Reynolds recalled few distractions or problems with on-lookers and visitors. He disagreed with the reports that scores of fans and observers dominated the daily shoot. He thought the set was closed to the public.

Gene observed himself that the daily activity of Boys Town remained normal. "Boys were doing their work. It was agricultural with cattle and crops, 4H type of stuff—a wonderful institution . . . many farm boys."

From Reynolds's observation of the location shoot, there was little security or police presence, and there was hardly a need for it. As for the residents who worked on the picture, Gene said: "The boys were very obedient and well behaved on the set."

Frankie Thomas thought them abnormally quiet most of the time, perhaps in awe of the film stars, perhaps told to cooperate fully with the people making the movie. "If you found the same number of kids in Beverly Hills, they'd be more talkative."

Watching the boys in the background, one of the other actors pointed out to Frankie that one boy had been involved in the notorious Eureka Bank Robbery of 1932 in Kansas that had been in national news. At that, Frankie recognized him immediately "as a charming, very nice boy, so well-mannered on location!"

The resident boys were always neatly dressed in immaculately clean clothes. They were not ragamuffins dressed in tatters, but as Frankie said, "Still, it was not like they could walk into Sardis." Norman Taurog selected at least two of these boys for additional work. First was the former mayor, Tony Villone. He had an interest, not in acting, but working behind the scenes. He wound up in Hollywood, and he worked at MGM for many years thereafter. He would return to Boys Town in November of 1940 as the Technical Director on the sequel, *Men of Boys Town*.

A second boy had acting aspirations. Taurog gave him a plum role in the film as Charley Haines, the boy who begged to enter the Town near the climax of the film when Father Flanagan stopped in midst of a crisis to listen to the boy's plight. Johnny Walsh passed his first screen test with flying colors. He starred with Father Flanagan in a seven-minute MGM documentary, narrated by Frank Whitbeck, called *City of Little Men*. He was brought back to Hollywood with the fifty-two boys who comprised the A Capella Boys Choir to film scenes in the Culver City studios.

For Gene Reynolds, the lead boy soprano from Hollywood, Raymond Chace, became a friend. "A wonderful kid, who sang Ave Maria." Gene recalled further with amusement, "Every kid from Boys Town sang as loud as he could. Tough little characters."

The Boys Town compound was an open campus with a major roadway on its perimeter where little Pee Wee was struck by a speeding car. During the shooting days, the village was overrun with visitors, tourists, and film fans. According to historian Tom Lynch, "Father Flanagan attended the filming everyday due to it taking place literally in his front yard. Many important guests came to watch the filming including the governor of Nebraska. In all each day around five thousand people from the Omaha area came to the village to watch the filming."

Despite the hospitality of Father Flanagan, he hated to see the large crowds damage his carefully manicured campus. Flowerbeds, shrubbery, and lawns were frequently trampled. Many sought a glimpse at how a motion picture was made. Dignitaries showed up as guests of Father Flanagan. A man attuned to the politics of his role, the priest was gracious and entertained many visitors.

Tom Lynch revealed: "The impact of *Boys Town* is still felt here in the village. Each year thousands of visitors tour the village with memories of watching the movie. Also the movie had the impact of making Father Flanagan the authority in childcare around the world. It is also surprising just a few years before the movie was made Boys Town was on the verge of closing. Due to the Great Depression and the Dust Bowl droughts, Boys Town was out of money and food. Father Flanagan made plans to close the home, but each week a donor would come forward to give Father some money and food. Just a few years later the name Boys Town and Father Flanagan were household names, and would evolve into an American institution."

At noon, because the weather was so hot, the cast and crew ate at folding tables out of doors each day while there. MGM catered their lunches on location. Frankie Thomas described, with slight derision, the usual luncheon fare under the cool shade of the trees. "We ate Santa Monica Seagulls from the catering. It was chicken, but not very good chicken. We had these things in containers, but I recall those seagulls. We all used to kid about it."

One of the resident boys who worked as an extra revealed a moment out of his lore of Hollywood. Charles Kopplin told how the two main stars behaved one time when Spencer Tracy sat down in costume to have his meal. Kopplin explained, "Mickey used to agitate him. They had this long table, so Mickey comes in (and sits) across from him and took off his shoes and socks." To make his appearance completely unappetizing, Rooney put his feet "right up in front of Tracy's plate. Oh, Tracy, was he burning a hole through it." The famous glare must have gone into overload.

Both actors were legendary for remaining in character, off the set during filming. This may well have been a case of Whitey Marsh trying to prove to Father Flanagan that a bad boy was present. Though Frankie Thomas didn't see Mickey pull this particular stunt, he agreed that pranks with Tracy at meals were likely. Spencer played elaborate practical jokes himself, but in his role of priest may have been at a disadvantage.

Both Rooney and Tracy were fast workers, and they did scenes in one take. Since neither liked to rehearse for a role, they seemed particularly fresh and spontaneous during their moments together. Preparing for a scene was easy for each because both disdained make up. They'd put on their wardrobe for the scene, had their hair combed, then dashed for the set.

Though Hollywood magic made it appear that the entire film may have been shot at Boys Town, the truth was far from that. A few scenes done in Nebraska were used in the movie. Total time for location shots consisted of about thirteen minutes of the full-length of ninety-three minutes. The outdoor sequences at Boys Town, and one shot of Union Station in Omaha, were the extent of location film work. Taurog and the stars worked on both Saturday and, in a social vein, on Sunday, always as representatives of their studio and the film industry.

A quick view of the Boys Town grounds and buildings in the film production included Frankie's explanatory guide scene at Boys Town, as Freddie Fuller. Blond and handsome, with enhanced eyes, Frankie Thomas admitted he wore eyeliner for his role. "That walking tour scene with Bobs, Mickey, Sid, and me, we did that in one morning, and it was a dolly shot. We worked quickly and without any problems. Yes, the campus was so spacious and looked like a fancy Ivy League college, but I never went into a single building."

His recollection may not be quite exact; Tom Lynch of Boys Town contradicted Frankie: "One of our former boys remembers the film people entering the buildings, and using the gym area for scenes. A scene from the movie shows Tracy walking out the front door of Father Flanagan's house." The Monsignor did not find school disrupted by the filming, but encountered a problem of his own in his office, which had a fine view of the grounds.

Taking it with a good-natured laugh, Father Flanagan was interrupted frequently while sitting at his desk. The movie's assistant director would call out to the priest through his open office window every few minutes. "Duck, Father. We're shooting the administration building and you're in the picture!"

Mickey Rooney remembered attempts were made to film inside the Boys Town gymnasium auditorium. Others recalled working at the Boys Town gymnasium because it had lavatories and a shower room the cast and crew were allowed to use. The building was constantly in use by residents. Being so handy, the members of the film company were granted use of the amenities.

On Sunday, July 3rd, Norman Taurog arranged for the choir scene to be vocally recorded. Edward Ward, MGM's musical director, was on location in Omaha for this purpose, and planned to record the choristers on Sunday afternoon without having them don white surplices and black cassocks to perform. This recording of the choir's rendition of "Ave Maria" was to be dubbed over the actual scene of them singing, dressed in their vestments, which was scheduled to be filmed later in the week on the same auditorium stage.

Weather outdoors had been unbearable during the previous week; without air conditioning, the small auditorium at Boys Town was sweltering. Ward supervised the hanging of heavy, sound-absorbing draperies from ceiling to floor, but the requirement for the sound recording trapped the hot, stale air in the auditorium, raising temperatures to 95 degrees.

Because the arrangement proved too hot for lighting and other camera requirements, they agreed to take down the drapery on the subsequent Wednesday, since the sound on that day would not be used.

Ward and Taurog presumed, incorrectly, that their recording equipment would operate properly. When Ward listened to the playback after the first attempt, the sound slipped on the wax-based disc half a note. Ward had to do it over. A second take was fouled up when the lead boy soprano found himself de-hydrating, losing his voice; he may have been suffering a bit of flight lag as well.

Young Raymond Chase had flown in the day before from Los Angeles where he'd been working at MGM, dubbing his voice for the 'boy' prologue in *Girl of the Golden West*, with Nelson Eddy and Jeanette MacDonald. Fully prepared, he fit in easily with to sing with the real boys of the Town and later told Gene Raymond how they made up for any deficiency in quality by the sheer volume of their voices.

Ward judged that the third recording attempt was perfect. However, during playback, the needle on the player kept repeating over a segment in the groove of the record. The wax had melted, owing to the high temperature. For a fourth time, the good-natured group sang "Ave Maria", yet again. Luckily, the sound equipment did not malfunction. It was synchronized to play over the boys when appearing in their full regalia.

On Wednesday, even without drapery, the makeshift indoor filming didn't hold up under the heat, and the entire choir was transported to Culver City several weeks later for re-takes under better conditions.

After this loss of two full days work, owing to the heat and its ramifications, Taurog asked Rooney to work on Sunday. Always a trouper, the dynamo agreed to perform. He did one of his hitchhiking scenes out on the roadway heading to Omaha. For most of Sunday afternoon, Mickey was filmed, sticking out his thumb at passing cars, trying to catch a ride out of Boys Town. As expected, many cars zipped right past, not slowing down enough to notice it was Mickey Rooney on the side of the road, waiting for a lift.

Like any movie fans, boys at the town were fascinated and surprised by the filming process. Back in 1938, this was especially true for the youngsters who had the chance to participate in a genuine Hollywood movie. Hank Avilla had a distinctive memory of Norman Taurog's occasional troubles. "Okay, this is going to be a take," he heard Taurog say. The entire group of boys settled down and ready for the camera to roll.

Hearing the cry of "Action!" Mickey Rooney came charging down one of the broad expansive paths. "About that time," related Avilla, "there's a great big sonic boom."

Taurog was stunned and cried out, "My God, what was that?"

In the nearby field was a whole row of cottonwood trees. One resident, named Al Witcofski, unaware of the shooting, was blithely blowing up stumps. "Anyway, you could see the stump going up in the air," laughed Avilla.

Taurog showed his patience and asked, "Do you mind sending somebody down there and telling him to wait for maybe an hour?"

Non-professionals are surprised at the slow pace, repetition, and deliberate nature of filmmaking. It seemed a boring process to many who viewed the arranging of lights and moving of equipment. One of the extra boys, named Ed Novotny, gave an especially accurate depiction of what occurred. "The movie crew would get their reflectors, wait for the sun to get in the right position. Then at a given point, you just had a certain pocket, window and at that time they would shoot. Then a cloud would come over and you'd stand there for half a day waiting and finally everything would get okay again or they would move around to the side of the building where the sun hadn't been and then they would go ahead and shoot."

Another common film technique is the Day for Night shot. This entails doing scenes in a shadowy moonlight that is the creation of lighting tricks. The scene is always shot in daylight. For Ed Novotny, he explained clearly his experience with the classic movie trickery. "They threw a canvas over it to make it night—spotlights and everything."

For former resident, John Anthony, who found himself in a few disparate scenes in the background, "I think the most interesting thing was all of a sudden you could pick out different scenes where maybe you saw yourself and then it was like a miracle because the fact that they had all these pieces and segments and then all of a sudden they put it together and here you got a beautiful movie come out of it. The filming of every scene wasn't very long. You think it would be a lot more to it to make the picture but it filled in somewhere along the line."

One of the most memorable shots was done at Boys Town. Immediately after Pee Wee was injured in the car crash and carried down the wide boulevards of the town by Spencer Tracy and a raft of boys, there was a prayer scene. Showing rows of kneeling boys, deep in prayer, Taurog had one of his most striking images. Mickey Rooney, bereft as Whitey, wandered past each row, alone and going in the wrong direction until he talked to the new mayor, played by Gene Reynolds, in the last row

Nowhere in the scene was Sid Miller, nor Frankie Thomas, who could not explain his absence from this pivotal moment in the story. Whatever happened to keep him out of this marvelous scene, Taurog found a look-alike actor, tall and blondish to kneel in the second row. It might have seemed like Frankie Thomas to the casual eye, but it wasn't.

Former child star Dickie Moore interviewed several juvenile actors about their work on *Boys Town*. Bobs Watson told Moore how he idolized Mickey Rooney, and was star-struck by the chance to work with him. He told Moore, "There was a scene where I get hit by a car and Mickey runs over and picks me up and he cries. I never felt so much emotion coming out of anybody. He was absolutely fantastic."

Shortly before his death Norman Taurog revealed an interesting aside about the making of the movie. He told Bobs what really happened and it was included in Moore's book *Twinkle, Twinkle, Little Star*. According to Bobs, Taurog took off the gloves after putting up with much of Rooney's shenanigans. "Years later Norman Taurog was living near where I was working, and he invited me to visit. Of course, we got to reminiscing, and Taurog told me what really happened when they shot that scene. Mickey had been acting like a spoiled brat."

Taurog continued to lambaste Rooney, according to Watson. The star had been giving the director considerable trouble, and Mickey said, "Well, I don't know whether I am going to do this scene your way or not."

Taurog replied, "Mickey, you can do the scene any way you want, if you want that little kid Bobs to steal it from you. He's giving you a run for your money. Just watch what he's doing. See if you can match it. I don't think you can, but you do whatever you want to." As a result of this, Bobs noted, "Mickey came through like gangbusters."

After the day's shooting, cast and crew jumped into the hired cabs and went to the Fontenelle Hotel. One cast member admitted, "We never saw anything of Omaha. Coming back at night all I saw were empty roads." *Per diem* vouchers from MGM allowed them to have dinner in any of the restaurants in Omaha. Those who were scheduled to do scenes the next day checked their lines and usually had an early night. Sunday was their own time, and many took the opportunity to have some fun for a while. Frankie said: "A lot of the fellas, mostly the technicians, went out on dates."

Over the Fourth of July, he noted how the girls of Omaha plagued the actors during those two weeks by sneaking into their hotel to see them. He said he'd been asked upon occasion to leave his room so his roommates could entertain, and also recollected that the local sorority girls put on a big dance party for the movie company. Normally reserved, the actor preferred to stay fairly much to himself; he was never really part of the youthful cast fraternity.

At Boys Town, Father Flanagan always scheduled a major celebration of the Fourth of July, and it was a special occasion in 1938 with the presence of major film stars like Spencer Tracy and Mickey Rooney. The cast and crew were invited to share the holiday at the village, rather than stay at their hotel in the city.

A bar in the Omaha hotel was a dangerous temptation for Spencer Tracy when he was away from home on a holiday, but surviving cast members never noticed an ambulance nearby, nor saw any medics on call at the Omaha location. The sole protector of the Oscar-winning star was Frank Whitbeck. And, the overwhelming friendliness of the village of little future men contributed to making Tracy feel good about his own work and the film they were making.

Before long, the location work at Boys Town was done and ready to filter into the pantheon of legend. No one could know that this movie would become a staple of the Golden Age. For most it had been just a job, however pleasant.

Frankie Thomas noticed on the last night, when they went to the train station for the long ride back to Culver City, that it was totally mobbed. As big, if not a bigger crowd than the horde, which greeted them upon arrival, was there to say goodbye.

"Many of the boys had someone at Union Station to say goodbye. Boys at the train station, we had a lot of beautiful gals from Omaha. There were many warm embraces and clinches. There had to be more going on over those two weeks than most people realized. If I had a camera, I could have caught pictures of so many guys, not just crew, embracing these girls whom they had come to know over the two weeks."

The cast and crew were back at MGM just a week after the Fourth of July.

7

THE BOYS AT METRO

Upon the company's return from Boys Town, director Norman Taurog turned up the pace of his work. He began to film the prologue scenes, encompassing the first forty-five minutes or so of the motion picture. Rooney and the other youthful actors who went to Boys Town were put on a three-week hiatus while a new group of boys depicted the early days of Father Flanagan in 1917 and established the reasons and issues behind his first Home for Boys.

Only Tracy, Hull, and Addison Richards as the Judge, would overlap both halves of the movie. Many moviegoers may not understand that seven years passed in *montage* of growth at Overlook Farm. The new young actors were the first ragamuffins who convinced Father Flanagan to start a home for wayward youth. The principal juvenile players included Mickey Rentschler as the elder, Tommy. The key role featured Martin Spellman as Skinny, who was a particular favorite of the priest.

Dore Schary's screenplay had been merged with Eleanor Griffin's story. The Schary storyline was dominating and sharply delineated, and it overwhelmed the early scenes of the picture. By casting the second half with name child actors of the era, MGM also gave the second half of the picture more prominence.

The screenwriter's own philosophy of movies as an entertainment medium was "of the people, by the people, and for the people. 'Of' in the sense of being about people, real people, whom audiences recognized as true; a movie script is more like the score of a symphony. The written notes of the symphony mean little until men play them in concert, and a movie script can be transferred from the paper to the screen only by the creative contributions of many hard-working and talented men and women. The motion picture is the most collaborative of all the arts."

Whatever changes to the script occurred upon return of the movie company from Omaha, Schary was completely out of the picture. Working under producer Harry Rapf, Schary clashed over a script idea and was summarily fired. Though he wanted to appeal to Metro bigwig Eddie Mannix, who liked and supported him, the production manager of the studio was away mourning his mother's death. The future winner of the story for *Boys Town* had been dismissed from MGM and cleared out his office.

Schary quickly learned about Hollywood. Scripts were not necessarily put on the screen as the writer envisioned his plot and characters. Boys Town was a classic example. "The continuity version is often the script account kept of the film as shot, with scene or line changes in it and would be different from the original numbers of drafts or final screenplays, (which also includes the occasional published versions, which are often different, too!)"

Not only would Schary be off the payroll while his screenplay was filmed, it's likely that two years earlier the odd mishmash of two stories, down-sized to half their original length, were glued together under the tutelage of Irving Thalberg. It was the fusion, which gave birth to the movie as it returned to the studio for its soundstage scenes.

The production of *Boys Town* took place during a new era at MGM. Everyone in the business still refers to Irving Thalberg as "the boy genius" who gave Metro its Golden Age, but by mid-1938, the studio was approaching its second sad anniversary of Thalberg's death. Some speculated the changes at Metro would be too much for Mayer to handle, and that his studio, without its artistic conscience, would fall into the realm of producing pictures on the caliber of the Poverty Row studios, like Monogram. That meant low budget and low quality. Still, in 1938, the influences of Thalberg still resonated from beyond his grave.

Although not an MGM contract player, Frankie Thomas spoke in reverent terms about the boy genius. "He was very conscious of art. He would buy properties not necessarily box office standouts. He did all the literary projects, like *Tale of Two Cities*. He did it again and again."

In a temperamental, emotional world, Thalberg seemed to be a glacier, removed and aloof. He had a royal presence. No one burst into his office unannounced, and he did not freely use vulgarities when they were commonplace among the studio folk. He had a puckish sense of humor, but seldom laughed. Once he took a script into the bathroom and promised the writers that, "I'll bring it all back."

Thalberg oversaw the major change in 1929 when he brought in a generation of "talking" actors into the new sound films. "It was a hard business with very nice people and many of them came from Broadway. A bunch came in 1929 and 1930 after the first talkie," revealed Frankie Thomas who also noted one of the giant schisms that dominated the business in the 1930s. "There is one variance from my view that everyone was nice. There was one group who resented anybody who came from New York. They were called the Coast Defenders. They resented the big money and the voices and the fact that we could play better. I ran into this with juveniles . . . especially the stage mothers."

Child performers ruled Hollywood in the summer of 1938. A generation had grown up and been discarded, with a new group of talented 'moppets', as the business called them, taking over. Jackie Coogan experienced replacement by Jackie Cooper, and Mickey Rooney overshadowed both. Growing older, these pint-sized thespians were faced with rejection and a shock to their alternately tearful or brightly smiling systems.

Their salaries were astronomical, and it was no wonder parents wanted their own talented youngsters to be 'discovered.' One central casting agency in Hollywood at the time reported that there were 1500 registered film actors under the age sixteen in the business. Of these, only a dozen were featured, and fewer yet made $50,000 per year.

Two boys to make a mark in the business were in *Boys Town*, and each represented a different end of the spectrum. Frankie Thomas, a trained stage actor, who at ten was a star on Broadway in *Wednesday's Child*, typified the imported New Yorker. Martin Spellman, a local boy from Culver City, enjoyed the legendary discovery, going from newsboy who sold magazines from a bag slung over his shoulder to the instant role of major film actor. The Cadillac of studios was Metro-Goldwyn-Mayer, where treatment and conditions purportedly was better than anywhere else in the business.

Frankie Thomas, who'd been at RKO and Universal, believed he was essentially a commodity to be "loaned out to another studio. My reaction to going to Metro was, 'Hey, I got a job.' It was like any trade. It was like being an electrician." To an untrained performer, like Martin Spellman, the chance to be a movie actor was a dream-come-true. He said: "I always find it hard to believe when these 'Hollywood Kids' complain about their 'lost' childhood. It was the best time I ever had!! Being a Movie Star was like being King. I loved it!"

Each boy had a career-altering encounter with Irving Thalberg in 1936. As Frankie recalled the young production head, "One thing about Thalberg is that he was very gentlemanly. Even as a kid, I could see how he was not much like others in the business."

When Frankie was shooting *A Dog of Flanders* at RKO, he was utterly confused by a sudden shutdown of production in the middle of the day, during pivotal scenes. "My mother and I were taken out to this limousine. We sped off the RKO lot and right through the main gate of Metro and did not stop for the guards."

For Frankie it was a first glimpse at how great the studio system was. Studio bosses could be some of the most powerful people in the state of California. "When Irving Thalberg wanted to see me, we stopped production on *Wednesday's Child*. It cost the RKO studio plenty, but it was MGM calling. I suppose this was all done as a courtesy from studio to another."

Frankie was immediately admitted to the main office building of the Metro lot. Though he was fourteen, he looked about ten, being so small. "We went to this large room and, even at my age, I recognized these were the five brains of Metro: Mayer and Thalberg and a few others (probably David O. Selznick, Howard Strickling and Eddie Mannix)."

No sooner had Frankie set foot into the room, than he found himself under the microscope. In particular, "Mayer looked at me and said, 'No, he's too strong'."

To his surprise, the others were not subservient men giving a cursory "yes," to the boss. Thalberg began to countermand Mayer. As he made a case for casting Frankie Thomas: "You should have seen him play a boy in a wheelchair. He can do it."

L.B. Mayer insisted, "No. No woman is going to feel sorry for him."

At that point, Frankie and his mother were ushered out of the office, returned to the limousine, and then went back to RKO to continue filming for the day. Three days later, Variety announced that Australian actor Freddy Bartholomew was signed to play the title role in *David Copperfield*. Frankie Thomas modestly conceded, "He was much better than I would have been."

After that incident, whenever a boy's part came up at MGM, Thalberg wanted to give the role to Frankie. "Mayer had a reputation for being very, very tough, but he knew enough to leave Thalberg alone. He produced a lot of good pictures. He was very artistic. Thalberg may have liked me, but it had something to do with the stage." Alas, Irving Thalberg's days at the studio were numbered as his heart condition continued to deteriorate and the producer's days were numbered.

In his first film role, discovered by Clark Gable, Martin Spellman performed with Spencer Tracy in several key scenes. Photo courtesy of Martin Spellman.

As for Martin Spellman, a chance to win a bicycle brought him to the gates of MGM in the summer of 1936. He was selling *Liberty*

Magazines at various government offices in Culver City. At age eleven, he too was extremely small for his age and seemed an overwhelmed waif, toting heavy bags of magazines on his shoulders. One day in an effort to make new subscribers, he went over to MGM, near his neighborhood.

"The only place with a lot of people that was close to us was MGM, Metro Goldwyn Mayer studios. They were about the biggest at that time. Their slogan was they had 'more stars than in the heavens'. If he could sell enough magazines, Martin figured he'd be in heaven with a new bike.

Though he rationalized he just walked into MGM by accident, it wasn't so, since the heavily guarded entry was notorious for turning away any unwanted visitor. The fate Martin made was by his own hand and design. "I think the real truth is that when I was standing there, watching people go in and out the electrically controlled gate, I realized the lady that controlled the gate was sitting up on top a high platform and couldn't see me if I just followed someone in through the door. I was small for my age. I know it sounds sneaky, but remember I am pretty desperate. My sales are down, and I have to win that contest to get that bike!"

So he just walked into Metro.

Immediately sales were brisk. Wherever he went, kind and friendly people bought his magazines. "It was heaven," he remembered. In one administrative building, Martin walked into a spacious and magnificently appointed office, but no receptionist was at the central desk. He merely strolled to the open doorway of a bigger office.

This was the recently designed set-up provided by Cedric Gibbons to make Thalberg appear isolated. The grandeur included high, beamed ceilings, a massive fireplace, oversized leather chairs and a desk covered with a two-inch thick glass.

At the end of the vast room, sitting at a big desk, was a small and frail, dark-haired man that Martin thought was very young to be in such a place. The man looked up to see this waif of a child peering at him from the doorway and invited Martin into his office. He asked why the boy was there.

Flashing his smile, the small boy showed the man at the desk his pack of *Liberty* magazines. He was selling them. The man at the desk "seemed to get a kick out of the fact that I got into the studios as they were heavily guarded." After that, the executive bought a magazine and "made me promise I would come to see him and sell him one each week. Now I was taught you always keep a promise so I don't usually promise unless I can keep it. But I saw no problem now that I had found this gold mine; so, I promised." Spellman sold all his *Liberty* magazines that day.

When Martin returned the next week, he was weighted down with 100 magazines. He carried fifty on each side, in canvas shoulder bags that *Liberty* provided. He had to balance the magazines on each shoulder, lest he tumble over. Much to his chagrin, bowed over under the load, the MGM electric gates did not open. No one came, and when he tried to shake the gate, the woman operator stood up and looked down from the top of the wall. She informed Martin he was not welcome.

"I was explaining why I had to go in, and I imagine too loudly, when this huge policemen in this general-like uniform came out of his office." This was Chief Whitey Hendry whose crack-force of security was the pride of MGM. These uniformed officers were like a village constabulary. Their order included saluting the stars in greeting.

An imposing man to a child, Chief Hendry called out in a booming voice. "What is the problem here?"

Martin was terrified and imagined being carted off in handcuffs. "But I stuck to my guns. I wasn't going to give up this gold mine without a struggle, and I also had promised to come back to the one customer." After some discussion, Chief Whitey relented: "I am going to let you go in this time, but unless you can get me ten signatures saying you won't be a problem, I won't let you in again."

Knowing no one on the lot, Martin figured his gold mine of sales was being shut down. His only hope was to go to the man who had promised to buy a *Liberty* each week. "I told him I was not going to be able to sell him a *Liberty* each week as I had promised. He wanted to know why. I told him I had to get ten signatures for Chief Whitey or I couldn't come back any more and that I didn't know ten people who would sign."

The calm executive smiled and scribbled a note, telling Martin: "You take this to Chief Whitey."

The boy protested, "That won't be enough. I have to get nine more."

Mr. Thalberg smiled again and said, "Just tell Chief Whitey that if he won't let you back in, I won't sign his paycheck anymore."

When Martin delivered the note, Chief Whitey Hendry opened it, read it, then looked at his pint-sized visitor and said, "Well, it didn't take you long to know some people in high places."

Martin acknowledged Irving Thalberg with the recognition, "I will always owe him."

Irving Thalberg and Louis B. Mayer attend a film Opening with Frank Whitbeck, obscured by microphone and serving as Master of Ceremonies. Whitbeck, a trouble-shooting executive, was a frequent traveling companion of Spencer Tracy. Photo from author's collection.

Though film actors respected MGM as a well-oiled machine, and the best work environment in the business, Frankie Thomas claimed it was "not all perfection." He cited an example of how MGM tried to make some actors into big stars and failed. "Mayer brought some Swedish girl, and they tried to make her a star," to no avail.

Frankie Thomas also mentioned Gene Reynolds as another attempt at star building. "They missed on Gene Reynolds. They pushed him on three pictures and failed." He also believed that Metro was less likely to let an actor stretch. If he were successful in one kind of role, there was little chance to break out.

Frankie worked with the likes of Ronald Reagan and Ann Sheridan at Warner Brothers, but said he never saw many of his coworkers socially and seemed genuinely unimpressed with the structure of the studios. "Metro was quite sincere about their feelings, but they were not well-oiled machines. I mention Universal was a bit more lackadaisical than the others. However, Mayer had a sense real sense of America. Nothing like that was innate in the people at the studio. His favorites were the Andy Hardy pictures, but that's what he wanted. Warners became extremely patriotic during the war, but that was already happening at Metro."

An incident that occurred may be indicative of Frankie's sourness about the studios, and MGM in particular. "I ran into Mayer. Judy Garland and I were having dinner at the Cocoanut Grove. She said something funny and we were laughing our heads off. She then whispered, 'Frank, Louis B. Mayer is at a table across the room.' And, she said we had to go over to him to prove that we were not drinking."

On the other hand, the newsboy about to become movie star was having a different experience with the MGM system. "Clark Gable and Myrna Loy were my favorites. He was as unpretentious and as friendly as anyone I have ever known. He always acted like we were best buddies and like he really enjoyed my visits and, of course, always bought a *Liberty*. Myrna Loy was like a second mother. She would sit and talk to me and ask me about everything I was doing. And most of all, she really cared! And you must remember these were the two biggest stars in Hollywood at this time. And they were spending time talking to a little newsboy."

Given the right to walk all over the studio lot, Martin began to frequent sound stages. "I went on all the sets and back lots. I knew MGM like the back of my hand. They had, I believe, 27 sound stages. Wardrobe departments, writers' offices and business office, I was able to wander the sets when they were empty and were kind of spooky to a nine year old but very interesting to see what they had been shooting.

I had the freedom to go any place, and no one bothered me. Of course, I was very careful not to be a problem. Almost everyone I met was wonderful to me. I knew and talked to almost every big star that MGM had. I became the studio mascot."

Martin visited Joan Crawford on the set and found her a concerned and pleasant woman. "She was always friendly and chatted with me. One day I came on her set. I was just starting out for the day, and it was my first call. It was raining very heavily. But I didn't mind. I have always liked the rain."

Trying to convince Miss Crawford to buy a magazine was not easy as she had her own independent thoughts on the matter. "She said she did not want me out in the rain. I said I was okay and didn't mind."

The star wanted to know how many magazines were in the canvas bags. "I told her I was just starting and had 100. She got her purse and gave me $5 and said, 'Just give them away and go home and get out of this rain'."

Martin attempted to talk her out of it, but she insisted. After thanking her, he started handing out free *Liberty Magazines* everyone on the set.

Miss Crawford's 'go-fer' on the set was a man who "always played mood music for her on a Victrola when she had an emotional scene. There was something about him. Flakey, I guess you would say. Anyway he came over afterward and asked me what I was doing."

The boy answered, "I'm handing out free *Liberties*. Miss Crawford bought them and told me to give them away."

He said, "You dumb kid, you can go sell them again and pocket the difference."

"No. They belong to her and I will give them away." Martin Spellman held to his code of honor:, "I thought she was a good person to worry about a little kid in the rain." Martin has long since heard all the terrible stories about the people in Hollywood and the terrible lives they led, but he never believed any of it.

A hundred movie stars milled around Metro on most days. Frankie Thomas said he seldom saw any of them. In a way Katharine Hepburn corroborated this years later when she admitted she could not find Spencer Tracy when she desperately wanted to meet him to ask him to do a picture with her.

Big stars did not hold much interest for Frankie. He did not ever seek them out and was not a movie fan *per se*. "As a matter of fact, I never saw Garbo. You didn't walk around to sightsee. If I went to the studio, I stayed in there. If you had any extra time, like if you were told to be back at two, then you might go off. It was at work. As far as Metro is concerned, if you ran into Gable at the studio, you would go home and admit that you were impressed."

Spellman was a fan, and he loved the atmosphere at Metro. He wasn't sure at the time who, exactly, Greta Garbo was, but he knew she was a mysterious and isolated person. Her trademark accent and a lament of wanting to be 'alone' were long established "She was supposed to be the top talent in Hollywood, according to MGM. Her sets were ALWAYS closed and NO ONE was EVER allowed to go on them. The new sets were much larger than the old sets, and it had a sign, 'Closed Set. No Admittance'. I guess I needed sales that day or something, but anyway I went on in. I guess the guard was going to the bathroom or something. So here comes Martin on this closed set to sell *Liberties.*"

Before anyone could stop the presumptuous boy, he went up to the beautiful lady sitting on a wide spiral staircase in a frilly hoop skirt, "just sitting alone."

Miss Garbo was on the set of *Camille*. Her co-star was Robert Taylor. "Before anyone could stop me, I asked her if she wanted to buy a *Liberty*. I guess they were all waiting for the explosion from this temperamental actress." Martin thought he heard people on the set gasp in horror.

She just patted her skirt and asked the little boy to sit down and said, "Please sit and talk with me." The leading lady smiled and wanted to chat with the newsboy. "So, I did, and we must have talked for twenty minutes. She was very nice. And, then they were ready to start shooting again so I had to get out of the scene. She smiled again. We said, 'Goodbye.' She was very sweet and kind to me. And I never saw her again. Somehow the gossip columnist Louella Parsons heard the story and wrote about it in her newspaper column. Mom kept the clipping in a scrapbook she made for me."

People at MGM began to take notice of this enterprising little boy.

Soon Martin became a special friend to Clark Gable and his companion, actress Carole Lombard. A small boy, he could see their devotion to each other. "When she wasn't working, she was always with him. They were not only lovers. You could tell they were good friends."

One day, when Martin was on the set, hanging around, he overheard Carole Lombard talking to Gable. "What are you going to get Marty for Christmas?" Not wanting to be eavesdropping, he moved away and did not know what they might do for him.

Later Martin learned that Gable had called his mother and asked permission to give the little boy a special gift. "There is a scene in my movie where a bunch of fans crowd around me, the pilot. It is just a crowd scene, and it will be shot at Burnable Airport at night. Would it be all right if we give Marty an extra part in that scene?"

Gable knew extras received $11 a day (a fortune to the average worker in the 1930s who worked all week for $5). Extras were compensated $25 if they spoke any lines. Martin said, "But, of course, this was a non-speaking part. I loved it!!!"

When they were shooting the scene a few nights later, director Victor Fleming said, "This scene needs a line. One of these fans should say something to this pilot, like ask him for an autograph."

Gable immediately said, "Great! Give it to Marty!"

Martin adored both Gable and Fleming whom he thought highly of. To the boy they "were both just real guys, not Hollywood types."

Spellman always thought: "These two plotted this one." Martin spoke the line, and the payment was $25, a sizable Christmas present.

"Myrna Loy who was also in the picture was overjoyed and promised me I could sit with her to see it at the studio preview. The movie was *Test Pilot* with Clark Gable, Myrna Loy, and Spencer Tracy."

Clark Gable's favorite co-star was Spencer Tracy with whom he enjoyed working, though they were not off-set buddies as the media portrayed. Gene Reynolds observed at the time, "Tracy was a warm guy, sympathetic." He believed that it was difficult for these high-profile glamorous stars to be friends in any normal sense. "All stars were incredibly dedicated to their careers, not necessarily in the best sense."

Gable and Tracy were quite popular with the workers at the studio. Crews liked both a great deal, but especially Tracy. "He was down to earth, but aloof and slightly amused by what he saw around him. He'd nod, and give you a good morning, but not hang around." Gable was much the same, but much more "gregarious."

Reynolds observed both frequently at the MGM Commissary. There was a strict system of who sat where. At one long, centrally located table, sat "cameramen, directors . . . the only actors ever to sit down were Gable and Tracy." It was an expensive seat. All those at this table played a game to pick up the tab for lunch or dinner. "They had an hour glass with dice in it. They'd spin it and the one with the low number had to pay for the table's lunch or dinner. You could go a month without paying or you could pay days in a row." The table sat thirty people most of the time.

A few weeks later Clark Gable called Martin's mother and said, "I saw Marty's scene and I had them cut it out. He has real talent and comes across very well on the screen."

Not quite grasping what Gable meant, Martin's mother said, "Oh, he will be so disappointed."

Known as the King around the studio, Clark Gable responded, "I know, but there is a very strict caste system in Hollywood, despite the exceptions you hear about occasionally. If you start off as an Extra, that is all you will ever be. I think Marty can do more. I am having a good agency, Conlon and Armstrong, contact you. It won't cost you anything, and they might get him some work."

Martin had a winning quality: it was his desire to catch the early worm. By his pluck and luck, he seemed to fulfill what Dore Schary always believed: "You need more than talent to get along in the picture business; you need either an alarm clock or insomnia. It's a business mostly of early rising."

Was Martin's discovery really just a case of coincidence? For two years he wandered around MGM and studied what he saw. "I also got to watch movies being made. I got to watch how the actors were instructed. How they did their lines: their mistakes and their good performances. I watched the top actors in Hollywood acting and how they performed in front of the cameras. It was wonderful training although I did not realize at the time that it was happening."

Tabbed for stardom by MGM, Gene Reynolds appeared as one of the mayoral candidates, the boy with the physical handicap. Photo from author's collection.

Gene Reynolds noted that, "Metro was like a family that quickly dissolved. Short lived and intense. Twelve hours per day acting and interacting. Then it's suddenly over and you go your separate ways."

Frankie Thomas took a cynical view, "MGM felt just like any other studio. The exterior of the studios looked like airplane hangars, one after another. But the restaurants, where they principally sold lunches, actually varied. Warners had a very posh restaurant where only the top people ate. I think it was called the Green Room or something." Frankie never recalled eating in the MGM Commissary.

For little Martin Spellman, MGM "was to start the magic time in my life."

8

SHOOTING THE
PROLOGUE AT MGM

While his crew filmed in Omaha, producer John Considine followed the usual procedure. He gathered the heads of key departments for a series of meetings. Called a set meeting, one usually took place in Cedric Gibbons's plush office. As the major art director of MGM, he oversaw the design and style of many key films from the Golden Age at Metro, influencing styles and furnishings across the nation. He had the total support, first of Thalberg, and later of L.B. Mayer. It was Gibbons who designed the Art Deco layout of the Commissary and gave Thalberg an office of enormous and regal proportions.

Before the location work finished its outdoor shooting, the production team needed to insure that special effects, montages, and miniatures were readied for use. The set breakdown was essential if Considine was to have the picture done by summer's end. He and his associate art directors, Urie McCleary and Edwin Willis, went through the script, scene by scene, making notations of all locales mentioned and the number of scenes to be played in each. They needed to see which sets should be constructed for use inside a sound stage.

Several key scenes in the prologue were done outdoors on the back lot of Metro with existing scenery and buildings. They had a generic city street that could be used for a fight scene with gangs of boys. They used a miniature for the train on which Whitey's brother would escape his prison guards, and they provided a snowfall to obscure scenes in the Christmas segments of the 1917 prologue.

Cast readings and off-camera rehearsals depended on the stars and the director. "While I was at RKO," said Dore Schary. "Out of the reading came a number of script changes. Some were merely changes in dialogue lines, which lay poorly on the actor's tongue or could be improved or dropped."

Call Sheets were created to determine which scenes came first, and this alerted departments as to what must be ready and when. Having endless details to oversee, like a general on a battlefield, John Considine made his contributions to the picture at this level. Among those sitting in on this meeting was Carl Roup, called the Major. Born in Idaho, he was long active in films, starting as a silent film extra as a boy. As a script supervisor, he enjoyed the trust of Tracy and Gable.

Friends recalled Tracy lauding the efforts of this job as requiring, "exactitude, discipline, careful study of each scene to be able to match cuts." Roup worked frequently with Tracy during the MGM years. Roup went to Boys Town, leading the technical staff, and he was instrumental in the speed of production. He could recall and note continuity details with an uncanny eye, saving many re-takes.

Martin remembered, "I only knew him as the 'Major'. He was very popular and well-liked by all. When I knew him, he was the 'script boy'. Actually a very important position and requires great organizing and memory skills. Everyone thought he would go far."

Taurog had less interest in this philosophy of improving performances and dialogue. Martin Spellman learned poverty row pictures were never concerned with accuracy of delivery. If the words were approximately said correctly, the take was accepted and became one of the daily rushes. "At Monogram if you got the words right it was a print. Many times I practically begged my director, Bill Nigh, to do a scene one more time to no avail. If you got the words right that was good enough. I realized later that Monogram was a mistake," lamented Spellman.

At MGM in the 1930s, under directors like Taurog, this steady pace became the preference of the studio bosses. Since Spencer Tracy abhorred re-takes, the match between director and star made for smoother production. Other stars required intensive attention at MGM, but it was Tracy's professionalism on the set that most won him support of the front office. It made them willing to put up with off-set difficulties. Martin revealed, "I was around Spencer Tracy many times, *Test Pilot, San Francisco, Boys Town*, and never saw him with a drinking problem. I would guess that, as good an actor as he was, he kept it separate from his work."

Dore Schary commented years later about his days as head of MGM, "Five minutes of screen time film in one day is considered fast." *Boys Town* did, at least, that much film per day while at MGM in order to achieve its record pace for finish. It was to be completed under its forty-four day shooting schedule. In contrast, the amount of film done at Boys Town in Omaha was small for the number of days on location.

Schary also explained the purpose of background shooting in one of his books on how the industry worked. "The Second Unit of a company, in general, picks up outdoor shots in which the principals either do not appear, or work sufficiently far away from camera to permit doubling." What happened on this production of *Boys Town* was Taurog directed all the principal scenes on location, and the second unit was used to create a ten-minute documentary entitled *City of Little Men*.

Though some might question the use of an inexperienced boy in this pivotal role, credit must be given to Spellman for the competence he showed to the production team. Like a child learning to speak a foreign language, Martin had an aptitude for performing and the ability to pick up the ambiance of filmmaking. "While I was selling magazines on those movie sets, I had to stop whatever I was doing and be very quiet when the director said, 'Action!' When he said that, no one moves except the actors on the set. Any noise might be picked up by sound equipment. And one thing that was a cardinal sin was to ruin a take." With his gregarious nature, Spellman was a natural for the job.

Shortly after Clark Gable arranged for an agency to take over Martin's career, there was immediate action in the boy's sudden movie work. After the release of *Test Pilot* in April, and Tracy's agreement to do *Boys Town* in March, John Considine began to surround his Oscar-winning star with the people he wanted from crew to cast.

If there were any who'd make Tracy feel comfortable, then there was a new addition to the production team. Tracy liked Major Roup as a script supervisor, and he trusted Sidney Wagner as a cinematographer. It may not have been hard for Martin's agent to find the lad a role in the Tracy picture, especially with Clark Gable in Spence's ear about their favorite newsboy.

The script supervisor on Boys Town was one of Tracy's favorites, Carl Roup, known by everyone on the set as The Major. Photo from author's collection.

The eleven-year-old boy knew only, "In a few weeks I got a small part in the movie *Boys Town* with Spencer Tracy. It was only three weeks, but at $75 a week, I couldn't believe it. It was in the very first part of the movie where Father Flanagan (Tracy) decides to help little street kids. I am one of the little street urchins."

Martin realized that at a major studio like MGM, "the scene was done again and again until the mood, the words, the acting, were exactly as the director thought they should be. At a major you might do a take twenty to thirty times until the phrase you were to say was exactly the way your character would say it, with exactly the right expression."

Henry Hull was, of course, wary of the children, more than Dave Morris, the character he played. The boys wouldn't have much to do with Henry unless the cameras were rolling. If he resented child actors, he never showed it, being a consummate professional. Martin and the other boys did not find him difficult or easy, helpful or mistrustful; he was there and did the role. The rumors around the set swirled vehemently enough that a child could hear them. "There were rumors that Henry Hull had a drinking problem and that this movie was his last chance. He never drank that I could tell on the movie."

The main actor with Martin in the opening scenes was Mickey Rentschler, a tall and dark-haired youth who played Tommy. Born in 1923, he was the eldest of the prologue boys, and the most experienced in films of the first gang of boys. He naturally became a role model and leader to youngsters like Martin who were feeling their way through the movie intuitively.

Mickey Rentschler had already worked with Taurog in the immensely successful *The Adventures of Tom Sawyer* earlier in the year. He would go on at Metro to appear in *The Adventures of Huckleberry Finn* with Mickey Rooney. Like many boys, he lasted through the war years, but by age twenty-one, after playing young soldiers in small roles, a part in *See Here Private Hargrove* in 1944, Rentschler left the movie business completely.

Closer to Spellman's age was Martin Graff, who played one of the small boys of the original five Father Flanagan took under his wing from the Judge. Graff suffered a short and troubled life. By the mid-1940s, he had been killed in a bank robbery. In some ways, the boys of the movie were as troubled as the real boys at Boys Town, and in many instances, there was less chance they could only receive succor, help, or attention, in the way Father Flanagan offered.

As an indication of the reality of the movie-making experience on set, Martin felt the Christmas scenes were particularly strong. Though it was summer in Culver City, indoors on the sound stage, Henry Hull as Dave, sprinkled with flakes, brought wrapped presents for all the boys. They sang "Silent Night," and artificial snow was everywhere.

Experiencing the impact of filming make-believe, Martin found the Christmas scenes particularly real. With fake flakes everywhere, it became easy for the young performer to act out a tearful, reaction scene, making a parallel to the Oliver Twist character clear and making Martin the front-runner for another Dickens re-make in London the following year. "I thought you said, if we were good, everybody'd help us," Skinny ruefully lamented, his eyes brimming with tears.

For the boy in his first major film, Spellman noted how the reality of the film's scene made him lose all sense of the days. "I don't know the time of year the movie was made. It always seemed to me to be late in the year, but I think that was because of the Christmas scenes."

Like millions of other fans of movies, Martin fell under the spell of the man who gave us the *ambiance* of MGM movies: Cedric Gibbons.

Outside of Thalberg and Mayer, Cedric Gibbons had the most influence on MGM movies and often is credited for the style and flavor of the studio's productions. Photo from author's collection.

Perhaps outside of Thalberg and Mayer, the most powerful and important figure at the studio was Cedric Gibbons. Starting in pictures in 1915 as a young man, he was Goldwyn crony from the start. Though from Brooklyn, he trained at the Art Students League in New York. His scenery was so stylish and modern that some laughed that in MGM crime films his 'bookie joints' were elegant. Gibbons's biggest claim to fame was the design of the Academy of Motion Pictures for Arts and Sciences' award, better known as the Oscar. His gold statuette was sleek, powerful, and classy.

During the course of his career, his name adorned over a thousand movies. He took all the credit, though he supervised a department with an iron hand. His particular interests gave MGM its distinctive movie style. Cedric Gibbons insisted on three-dimensional sets, eliminating the backdrop as a painted flat surface. And, his peculiar color fetishes became legendary, as he decried green and red together in any situation. He loathed wallpaper, and he would not countenance MGM film sets with rooms so debauched. He preferred brightly lit rooms, offering the audience softness and warmth. Fluted woods and rococo woodwork were his staples.

Known as a fop by many, he wore ascots and gray gloves with his gray homburg. It's how he came to work each day for decades. And, he was about to design Boys Town in the MGM manner. Hard times and slum conditions would not deter Cedric Gibbons. He knew what the sets must convey.

The Workingmen's Hotel in the movie, haven for hoboes, derelicts, and homeless men, was likely one of the smokiest sets Gibbons would allow. Behind the smudged focus, the refuge he provided Father Flanagan was clearly a building that once enjoyed a glory in its better days. A closer look at the halls filled with men drinking coffee and playing checkers, revealed a former restaurant or long-ago elegant Victorian saloon, fallen into hard times. Its first floor windows looked out onto the traffic in the streets. The glass panes are stacked with a darker color (likely green) on the bottom.

The rooms enjoyed partitioned floor space where tables could be arranged in intimate configurations. The walls were wainscoted panel with intricate design. Columns separating rooms were clearly mahogany pillars. In nearly the same fashion, the Bishop's office was without wallpaper and features oak desk, a muslin curtain allowing in ample sunshine. It was appointed simply in reverence, shadows cast by the brilliance of sunshine entering.

In some ways the pawnshop of Dave was busy with neat rows of clutter, with stacks of furniture (chairs and tables) and the walls are adorned with neat shelves, featuring items grouped together in similarity. When Father Flanagan came to retrieve the boys, Dave had put them neatly in a row, handcuffed together. And the judge's chambers were bright, displaying a surprising amount of expressionistic light stretching across the soft white back walls.

In the German-American civic center Father Flanagan rented for his first five boys, Gibbons inserted his elegant architectural styles. When first seen, the dilapidated house seemed in disrepair, but was a large spacious mansion. By the scene of their first Christmas, the main rooms are warm in sharp contrast to the cold snowy conditions outdoors, and the depressed emotional state of Father Flanagan who has found few supporters for this humanitarian operation.

The main room was sunken from the foyer, a great open space with fluted archways in either direction. There was a carved mantle around the large fireplace, which warmed the environs for the boys, upward of twelve.

A year later, a long shot of the front yard shows dozens of active boys, all cleaning and sprucing up the place. When Dave entered, the immense size of the place was evident. Though beds have filled every space for a hundred boys or more, the cream colors of the archways and design of the appointments gave the house the feel of an antebellum mansion out of *Gone With the Wind*. Gibbons stressed the front door in brightness, with etched glass. Housing more boys than it could possibly, the plot required Father Flanagan to find bigger digs, but his housing for the boys was nothing short of a well-to-do country club.

After the montage sequence, Father Flanagan's Overlook Farm turned into Boys Town. Gibbons created the interior of the pastor's office on the Metro lot. He designed Flanagan's personal quarters (resplendent with modern divan) and the assembly hall for the choir, the boxing match, and the elections, using an old gymnasium at MGM. Whether Gibbons gave any consideration to Father Flanagan's own design of Boys Town remained unclear. Expressing his taste for comfort and status, it was no wonder that actors like Tracy preferred to stay on the soundstage, rather than travel to real locations.

Gibbons had access to the MGM file photo of Father Flanagan's office in 1937. Though not greatly revealing, the photograph indicated a small space that was crammed with documents and office files. When Cedric Gibbons created the office for the movie version of the cleric, the room was spacious, having at least three wide windows providing great illumination. Shadows of tree limbs cast themselves on the walls.

Loving cups adorned cabinets, and walls were covered in a variety of pennants, photos, and memorabilia of 'Boys Town' sporting events. The highlight of the room for Pee Wee was also one of Gibbons's favorite furnishings: an ornate, oversized, plush leather chair. The room would never be mistaken for cluttered.

Places like Whitey Marsh's cold-water flat, where Father Flanagan first encounters him, were cozy, with checkered tablecloth. Walls were covered with snapshots, but artfully arranged. The one-room was ergonomically efficient, yet darker than most Gibbons sets—and windowless too.

For the judicial hearing at Boys Town, the room developed by the Art Department was a small library or conference center. The wall-to-floor bookcases likely held several thousand leather-bound volumes. This room was likely based on a photograph taken by Eleanor Griffin during her visit in 1937. The real library likely held more books than the movie version. The hallway served in several capacities, as the waiting area for the judicial hearing, as the place leading to Father Flanagan's office in one scene, and to the hospital where Pee Wee recovered in another.

Two odd sets deserved attention. First, during a scene in which Whitey was wounded during a bank robbery, he was left in an alley in Omaha. It was stark and grey, but in no sense dirty or seemingly ever used. Its shadows were grainy and cement and granite dominated the atmosphere. When Whitey's brother deposited him into a church nearby, there was no contrast whatsoever. It almost seemed as if Whitey were still in the alley.

Second, the climax of the picture featured the entire student body of Boys Town, led by Father Flanagan, storming the bank robbers who were holed up in nearby rural location. The building was meant to be a deserted, fancy restaurant. It served as a setting foil to the Workingmen's Hotel, abandoned by Father Flanagan for his higher calling to start a boys' home. The town boys smashed open this closed business to save their own village.

Directors or producers who had a dispute with Gibbons over his sets were summarily dismissed. Most knew enough to accept his quirks and his style. His staff made models and gave him blueprints of every *Boys Town* set, and he approved each. Gibbons himself never picked up a pencil, and Mayer never overruled Gibbons. When MGM made *Boys Town*, it was in the Gibbons utopian style.

Taurog was a company man in the truest sense. Like L.B. Mayer, his politics was extremely conservative, and he performed civic duties on behalf of MGM. Though Norman took time during production to make an appearance at the Culver City Crime Prevention Club on one Monday night, he was always conscious of bringing the picture in on time and under budget. He preferred no readings, few rehearsals. Right before filming, he held quiet discussions with actors, letting them know how he wanted the action performed. In those days at Metro, the action was put on film as soon as possible.

The first half of the Boys Town film was done at Culver City on the backlot. Here, Spencer Tracy as Father Flanagan struggles with Skinny (Martin Spellman). Photo courtesy of Martin Spellman.

Frankie Thomas admitted he never really mingled socially with the technical people or the crew, and he believed, "As craftsman, they were as respectful of the actors as we were of them. A good cameraman could make or break you. The other side of the camera stayed there. They did their jobs, and we did our jobs. They were two different worlds."

At Metro, especially, came a sense from all who worked on a motion picture to "get in there and get it done right." Everyone wanted to produce the best film they could possibly, and they all put their considerable talents into the job.

For some performers this was the biggest budgeted film they had worked on. From its initial concept as a B-level Mickey Rooney picture, the entire project had edged up on the importance scale at MGM. John

Considine prepared to do a film that was suitable as a follow-up to *Captains Courageous*. Frankie Thomas thought it might be a good picture, but he was already thinking about going back to Warner Brothers to co-star in the *Nancy Drew* series starring Bonita Granville. For him those episodes were just entertainment, not genuine acting. "When I went to the movies, I always paid my 25 cents . . . If an actor was pretty good, I'd watch a little closer."

Martin was unaware of the reputations of the people around him. He'd certainly heard that Taurog was noted for being an excellent director with children. It put him somewhat at ease in his first project, but Spellman was completely unaware of the history and background of his fellows on the shoot. "I didn't realize until I read Jackie Cooper's book that Norman Taurog was his uncle. In it he really denounces his uncle for telling him his dog died to get him to cry in a scene. I thought typical Hollywood ingratitude. His uncle was trying to get him to act. Typically, Cooper indicates he was traumatized by this terrible event."

Crying scenes were always difficult for nearly every child performer. The means to cause their tear ducts to open were always dubious, yet thought of as merely part of the professional technique. Notions of emotional abuse were dismissed and a generation away; this was the world of make-believe. Yet, for an untested actor, like Martin, the script detailed at least two moments when he was required in close-up to shed tears. It began to worry him.

"Skinny, my part, comes into the saloon where Father Flanagan is trying to save some drunks and is sobbing, telling him that his brother has just been arrested. It is then that Father Flanagan realizes that he should be helping kids with a future rather than drunks with no hope. I had read my part of the script, and I could see no way that I was just going to be able to start crying on cue."

Unlike Jackie Cooper, Martin trusted Norman Taurog and came to think of him as a great and underrated director. After telling his mother of his insecurities about crying, in all likelihood she conveyed this to Taurog. Martin had expressed his reservations, "Mom, I am not going to be able to do that scene right."

For the day of the filming, Taurog had already made a plan. He knew Tracy didn't want to re-do a scene several times because of a child unable to perform correctly. It was imperative for the director to wring a performance from Martin in one take.

"When the time came, Mr. Taurog had noticed how close my Mother and I were. He asked her if she would leave the set that day. I don't know if he told her what he was going to do or not. I suspect not."

Taurog certainly trusted his own abilities to inspire his juvenile actors. When he had the scene in the Workingmen's Hotel all set up, with Father Flanagan discouraged about working with derelicts and drunks, little Skinny was to charge into the center in a crying panic. Cameras were ready, and Spencer Tracy was standing there, awaiting the big moment.

The director took Martin to the outermost edge of the set and clearly started his impassioned pep talk with: "IMAGINE that when your mother left the set today she was hit by a car. *Imagine* this as clearly as you can. Now *imagine* that I am telling you that the hospital called and she is dying and we are not going to be able to get you there in time . . ."

Putting himself into the mode of imagination, Martin's tears flowed as he imagined this terrible scene. Taurog yelled, "camera/action."

Martin said, "I was crying as hard as I could. And, he pushed me onto the set where I run blubbering to Father Flanagan.

"At all times I knew we were pretending, but I couldn't stop crying, just imagining that scene."

Whether some would consider this as heinous as Taurog's manipulation of Jackie Cooper may be a subjective opinion. In the estimation of Spellman, Taurog did what a good director needed to help his actor perform what they all agreed was needed. "I don't know if he changed his style because of that (earlier episode on the set of *Skippy*) or whether Jackie Cooper wasn't listening very closely." Martin speculated, "Maybe he learned from the Jackie Cooper incident OR maybe Jackie just chooses to forget, but he, (Norman Taurog) clearly stated let's *imagine* this scenario and quietly spoke to me."

Whatever unfortunate view has been ascribed to Taurog because of Jackie Cooper's damning story, Martin remains "suspicious of Jackie's version. It is very self serving and is more of the 'Poor Little Hollywood Kid'."

Martin's costume included a cap pulled down over his ears and with the brim rakishly off-center. It was in the Horatio Alger mode of street urchins. "I was never quite sure who decides what the actors wear. I don't know if it is the Director or the head of Wardrobe Department or a joint decision. The actor is sent to wardrobe and that is what you are given for that scene or that movie. I think the cap was some kind of symbol that was originally quite 'posh,' but when discarded as out of style, (by the elite) and was picked up out of the trash pile and worn by the street kids." Martin himself wore it the way he wanted, which gave his character a distinctive style.

The other key scene Martin filmed was an outdoor street brawl, in which a running passerby popped Martin on the nose by as Father Flanagan (Tracy) held him tightly. "The scenes I had with Spencer Tracy were always one take. He knew his lines and I knew mine. I don't think he was being aloof as much as he was trying to stay in character. He was kind and priestly."

One of Spellman's bits of memorabilia from the movie is "a photo of Spencer Tracy and me that kind of personified the movie and was used quite a bit in the original promotions (which didn't hurt my career). Father Flanagan is kneeling and holding the crying little ragamuffin (Me). I was very lucky, in that one of the still pictures they used to advertise the movie was a picture of Spencer Tracy standing with one of the little kids as if against the world. That picture was seen everywhere. I was the little kid he was standing with. It gave me great exposure."

Working at Metro, Martin saw less of his co-workers on the film than he had as a newsboy. He did see Mickey on the lot several times, but had no meetings with Frankie Thomas, Sid Miller, or his foil in the second half of the film, Bobs Watson. "The kids in the prologue never knew the kids in the second part. We shot the prologue in three weeks as I recall. And when we were done, they started." Martin never had much chance to sample the MGM Commissary's legendary food. Though Gene Reynolds raved about their chicken soup, Martin went there only once, "and I don't even recall what I ate." Apparently the unknown ragamuffin actors in the prologue were given box lunches on the set.

As for the usual place for actors to chat, the dressing room, there was a larger room, not so private, for the featured players. He shared that space with the other boys from the first half of the film. Frankie Thomas, Sid Miller, and Bobs Watson, shared the same room when they rejoined the picture after their hiatus.

Martin modestly apologizes, "None of my movies except *Boys Town* and *Beau Geste* were classics, and all are terrible compared to the movies of today. At that time they were okay."

Spellman may be overly modest about his movie years, "After *Boys Town*, I went on to other studios but never returned to MGM. It was kind of like leaving Oz with no way back." Almost to prove the theory Martin had lost his magical world, he appeared with the canine star of *The Wizard of Oz*. Little Toto yapped at the heels of Martin in the movie, *A Son of the Navy*. In its own way, working with Toto was the central metaphor of his film career. They trudged down the long road, looking for home.

Though Martin believed the picture was old-fashioned and "pretty corny," he gave a convincing and amusing performance as an orphan boy, playing mistaken identity to his advantage. The most delightful part of the picture was his co-star. "I loved Toto! We had instant love. I really missed him when the picture was done." The shoot for this major film was a mere three weeks at Monogram. And, at the end, Martin had to say goodbye to Toto because the world of motion pictures never allowed lasting ties. Everything was ephemeral.

Of this period of his movie star life, Martin was realistic. "I made several more movies. It was wonderful and awful. All of those parts coming at the same time and I could only take one! I wanted to take them all . . . It was the most fun I had ever had and the money was incredible. I got $500 a week for *Beau Geste*. Donald O'Connor and I had the same agent. And he, the agent, swore me to secrecy because Donald only got $350. This was in a time when the average workman's salary was $25 to $30 per week."

Martin took a contract with Monogram, rather than one of the big studios. Whether his career path would have differed at MGM, is open to speculation. Monogram was pleased with his success in pictures like *I Am a Criminal*. "They signed me to a five-year contract. They were going to make several movies with me in England. The first year I got $150 per week and Mom got $50 just to drive me around and to school. It went up a great deal each year. It had yearly options."

Always small for his age, by the time he reached thirteen-years old, he was able to pass for much, much younger. "I actually looked only about 10." It was this factor that began to change, and Martin's career took a turn downward. Having left the nurturing and supportive world of MGM, he had cast his lot with the less reliable Monogram. "Just as I thought I was going to England, we had taken our shots, to star in *Oliver Twist* for Monogram, World Ware II started in Europe. I will never forget Scott Dunlap calling me in with tears in his eyes, saying they were not going to renew my contract as they were counting on me making movies for them in England."

Whatever career advice he was receiving, the results were not positive. Instead of seeking out work with one of the major studios, he was working with small-time producers who made a film, tailored to Martin, at Crescent Lake, near Arrowhead. As an indication of how a child actor could lose control of his own life, Martin was never told the name of movie he was making. Everything was banked on the viability of Spellman as the star. Martin's billing at Monogram was "Big Star," according to the Publicity Department.

The producers went into Monogram and said, "We have this movie that we have made with your star Martin Spellman and we will sell all or part to you." Monogram declined to have any part of this motion picture, which caused the producers to file for bankruptcy almost immediately. Whatever group this was, Martin had been sold a bill of goods. "I didn't know this was to be the end of my career."

Confused by the turn of fortunes, Martin thought his career concluded, owing to the War and his inability to film in London. Some years later, watching one of his later movies on television, he could see why they had not renewed his contract at Monogram. He understood why there were yearly options. "I had become a teenager! No longer a cute little kid but an awkward gawky teenager." The contract was designed to terminate when the boy turned into a taller, leaner, less winsome performer. Martin was no longer a moppet.

For someone like Frankie Thomas, this adolescent phase went into a holding pattern. Whereas Martin was done by mid-adolescence, Frankie boasted, "To have a young face is not a curse. If you're in your twenties playing teens, you play the role. If you look young, it might make your career longer. Who were the actors who played juveniles longer than anyone else? Richard Crenna was one, but the number one was Frankie Thomas. I was 33 and still playing juveniles."

Martin became close pals with Sabu, whose career suffered with the onset of adulthood, though he stayed with the movie business. "I made in all ten to eleven movies during this time period. It was the best time of my life. I loved being a 'star'. I wasn't to be one long enough to get bored like some of the stars I knew. However, I don't think I ever would have. It was just heaven to get paid all that money to play act."

Martin, all these years later, expressed disdain for the Hollywood child stars who complained about their life in movies and how it robbed them of something special in their childhood. "That may be true for them, but for me it was the best thing that ever happened to me. I loved every moment of it."

Using the seminal MGM movie that expressed the magic of Hollywood with the romanticism of childhood, the crowning achievement of Cedric Gibbons's Art Department, Spellman compared his life to that on the Yellow Brick Road with Toto. It seemed most appropriate. "It was like being in the wonderful land of Oz. The downside is, it is like having been to Oz, knowing it is there and not being able to find your way back. The rejection is very hard to take. It improved my life and my family's in just about every way. And I loved acting, still do. I hated the rejection!"

9

SHOOTING THE
SECOND HALF AT MGM

"Tracy just won an Oscar and was now playing opposite a boy who was like a midget. Imagine that! But the boy was the #1 box office draw!" Such was the assessment of Frankie Thomas.

After a three-week hiatus, the juvenile actors who filmed in Omaha at Boys Town were back to finish the interior shots. By now Mickey was utterly convinced that MGM had a perfect vehicle for its two brightest stars. He returned to the set with a renewed vigor to finish the filming in a record amount of time. Taurog, Tracy, and Rooney, were all one-take experts.

The script began to impress Mickey. "Sid played Mo Kahn, the Boys Town barber. What was a Jewish kid doing in a place run by Father Flanagan? Well, that was part of the charm of *Boys Town* and part of the charm of the picture: Catholics and Jews, friends together. Schary gave Father Flanagan a Jewish friend, a pawnbroker (played by Henry Hull) who believed that Boys Town was worth backing. So a Jewish moneyman was helping a Catholic priest; they were working together on goodness and justice. Ecumenically speaking, we were about thirty years ahead of our time."

Sid Miller teased Mickey that he could turn it off and on "like a faucet." And, not a shrinking violet during most of his life, Rooney himself later wrote: "As Whitey Marsh, the tough kid who gets religion, I stole the show." He liked to take good-natured kidding from Sid with

---

their hidden compliments. Mickey explained, "This nonchalance was all calculation on my part.

"During breaks in the shooting, I made it a point to clown around with whoever was on the set, telling jokes to the camera crew, playing the piano along side Sid. Then when the director called, I'd throw a gag over my shoulder and time my approach to the set just as the camera was ready to grind away. I did this to throw myself into a state of shock. It was like running a car in high gear, then suddenly shifting to reverse. It was an awful wrench and it busted me up a bit inside, but it got results."

Frankie Thomas concurred, "Mickey comes across as overwhelming, but he is very professional, and he and I never had a problem in the world." Having expert supporting actors helped Rooney as well, explained Thomas. Sid Miller was not just a hanger-on or member of the entourage. "I knew Sidney Miller quite well. He knew his stuff." By the time they had returned from Boys Town, they'd become an ensemble, like a theater troupe that had been working together for years.

"Right from the start it was not a hard role to play. My character, Freddie, was against Mickey. He was straightforward and ready to take care of people. He (Freddie) was an easy role to play because Mickey helped."

Sid Miller made himself indispensable to Mickey and was a regular face (like Gene Reynolds) in all the Andy Hardy pictures. Sid recalled, "I got to know Mickey very well. From that a friendship developed that's lasted ever since. Also, (we had) a professional relationship. I was with him in all those great Garland and Rooney musicals. I was with him in *Boys Town*, and we've even written some songs together, one that wound up on the *Hit Parade*."

One of the secrets of the enduring friendship between Sid and Mickey was that Sid was able to see the sensitive side under all the bravura that blinded most who ran into Rooney. "My first impression of Mickey was that he was very tough . . . just like the kid he was playing, but really talented. He did his lines well, always knew them, and he was one of the few actors I've ever known who could cry on cue without any artificial means. He had tremendous concentration when he was in front of the camera. If you didn't know anything else about Mickey, you could sense that he was going to be a big star someday."

According to Arthur Marx who wrote a comprehensive biography of Rooney, the major irritation and frustration for the young star was the fact he was not growing much. To Mickey's consternation, at twelve he was four inches shorter than the average eight year old. "He made up in toughness what he lacked in height." If anything would send him off into a sulk or fury, it was a joke about his height. There were times he became so belligerent he would fight. Sid concluded that some of his feistiness and hostility came from his mother who was "always on the set with him, just as my mother was. Nell wanted to make sure that Mickey was up there in front, doing what he was supposed to be doing, stealing the scenes from the older actors. Her boy was the best. He got his drive from her. Not that he needed to be pushed. It was built in."

One great reason for friendships among many of the juveniles was music. Mickey played the drums and composed, and it was an era when musicians like Gene Krupa were popular. If any of the child actors were talented musically, he or she had a niche in the group. Many parties were centered on musical talent. For Mickey and Sidney, whenever there was a lull in filming, they'd head over to a corner of the giant soundstage where an upright piano could usually be found. They'd work together on songs. It was the glue to their friendship, being collaborators. One witness said: "You rarely saw one on the studio lot without the other."

Sid was on the set at Metro, watching Mickey, or waiting for Mickey to do his work. "This day I wasn't in the scene. In my spare time I was working on a song with Mickey called "Love's Got Nothing on Me". That day Mick was doing a big scene with Spencer Tracy, when I walked onto the set to watch." Miller recalled it was one of the climactic moments wherein Tracy told Rooney, "You're no good, Whitey. You're a bad boy. I've been able to handle bad boys, but you're the exception."

The scene required Rooney to plead a highly emotional pitch for the priest to let him stay at the village. Mickey implores, "The guys are beginning to like me. Let me stay in Boys Town. I'll be good. I promise."

Sid's memory of the scene was vivid because of Mickey's performance. "At that point the script called for Mickey to start crying and keep it up through the remainder of the scene. Mickey was so touching he had everybody on the set in tears—the grips the cameraman, as well as Norman Taurog, the director.

"After the take, Mickey spotted me standing on the side and rushed over. 'Hey, Sid,' he said, 'I've got the bridge to the song. Listen to this.' And he pulled me over to the piano and started playing and singing the song we were working on. In the middle of this, Taurog came over and told Mickey that he'd have to do the scene again."

Rooney took umbrage, snapping at the director with his traditional on-screen scowl: "Why? I thought I was good!"

"Mike shadow . . ." Taurog explained.

Sid could tell from Mick's reaction how unhappy he was when faced with doing something unpleasant. "(He) took a deep breath and agreed to do the scene again. It must have been a four minute scene, and this time Mickey did it better than the first time. The tears started rolling down his cheeks in the exact same spot. It was like he'd been able to turn on a faucet. Everyone around was crying again."

Then Taurog yelled, "That's great! Cut. Print."

Mickey rushed back to the piano and started singing again with Sid.

When Dickie Moore wrote his autobiography and analysis of what it was like to be a child star in the 1930s, he admitted, "Mickey Rooney, for many years the king, was, as usual, a law unto himself. Once his career was launched, Mickey ran the show himself, starting at age six. By a substantial majority, our peers consider Mickey to be the best actor of us all . . . then as well as now. But off the screen they found him harder to take."

On the surface, everyone socialized with Mickey, laughed and enjoyed him. Yet, his arrogance created a deep-rooted hostility among the peers of juvenile stars. Few actually considered him a friend. Some, like Jackie Cooper, were considered arch-rivals.

Stage mothers kept their children from Mickey's influence. Cooper said in his own autobiography: "Even if he'd wanted to be friendly with me, my mother wouldn't have tolerated it because she believed he touched pee pees with girls, and she didn't want any of that when I was thirteen." Former child star Jackie Coogan made the comment: "Mickey around guys is a pain in the ass. He's got a great sense of humor, and he loves to put on the paper hats and lampshades. He's the life of the party."

One of Mickey's regular costars, Ann Rutherford summed it up best: "Everybody thinks we were such swingers. Oh, no! Except for Mickey Rooney. He was a swinger."

Filmed at the MGM studios, the election for the new mayor of Boys Town involves Gene Reynolds, Frankie Thomas, and Mickey Rooney. Spencer Tracy breaks up a potential fight between Rooney and Thomas. From the collection of Frankie Thomas.

Whatever sparks flew onscreen and off between Tracy and Rooney, there was respect from the juvenile star in the form of his attention to the veteran star's work ethic. If Spencer Tracy played a scene without Rooney, the young costar always stood behind the cameras, intently studying every move and nuance of the performance.

Rooney said in a tribute to Tracy long after his death, "When he talked to you, he looked directly into your eyes. He talked only to you. That's the mark of a great actor . . . listening only to you, then bouncing the remainder of the scene back to you." Spencer Tracy never made a comment publicly about Rooney.

For Gene Reynolds, who saw them up close, "Rooney and Tracy got along. I think Tracy was bemused by Rooney's antics. He was very cool and never became too emotional. But they never had lunch or were social. They went their separate ways. Tracy was not the sort who would clash with anyone. He was not a man who was easily upset. He was a great guy. There was no tension around him." In confirmation of this, Henry Hull said: "Rooney was a lot like Spence. He kept to himself, and they'd didn't have much truck with each other off camera."

Gene also saw that Tracy was "very kind and encouraging, but you didn't have much conversation with him off camera." Others were overwhelmed by how he looked at the other person in his scene. One said, "You felt riveted. There was no place to hide." In Sid Miller's opinion, "Tracy was the best listener in the world. When I did a scene in *Boys Town*, I swear those eyes bored into mine. I also did a scene with him in *Men of Boys Town*. The cameraman said, 'Spence, will you cheat your look to Sidney's right ear.' He refused. He wouldn't look away from my eyes. If they wanted his full face, they were going to have to bring the camera around. A lot of stars wouldn't stay on the set when your close-up was being shot, but he would."

Others who co-starred with Tracy over the years also offered a litany of praises. Frank Sinatra quoted Tracy as saying, "people should read lines as natural as in a conversation." One of Tracy's famous rules of acting was conveyed to Sinatra, "The only thing about acting you need to know is to know your lines, hit your marks, and be on time."

Another co-star, Joan Bennett, from *Father of the Bride*, another movie resulting in Tracy's Oscar nomination, "He didn't like to rehearse or to retake a scene. He said a line like it just popped into his head." As for his one-take perfection, the director of *Bad Day at Black Rock* and *Old Man and the Sea* saw the professionalism. John Sturges revealed: "He never muffed a line." The reason for this was, in Sturges view: "off stage as well as on . . . The part was always within him . . ."

The two people closest to him in his life were Robert Wagner, who became a surrogate son and protégé, and Katharine Hepburn. In Wagner's assessment, "He was always in character. It was inside. He changed my attitude about work and my responsibility. He put his arms around me and told me, 'You can do it'." Miss Hepburn once asked him why he always looked down before a scene and received a matter of fact response: "Well, I want to find my marks so I don't have to do the scene again. That's why I look down."

After returning from Boys Town, it was apparent the studio had been impressed by the good behavior of Tracy while working on location. Some may have attributed this to the daily socializing with Father Flanagan. Whether the idea came from Frank Whitbeck or someone else, the studio decided to hire on a local priest as Technical Advisor for the film.

Co-star Henry Hull revealed, "We had a technical advisor on the set, a young Catholic priest, name of Father John O'Donnell, and

Spence spent a lot of time with him talking about a lot of church stuff I didn't understand. But I remember one argument they had about who was who at the Last Supper, and Spence was using baseball lingo to describe the Apostles—like Andrew was a singles hitter, but Peter was a guy who could play cleanup and knock the ball out of the park." The studio had found a cleric with whom Tracy enjoyed chatting. For every film in which religion was an aspect of the storyline for Tracy, Father O'Donnell was the official MGM wanted for the job.

Gene Reynolds had already done a picture with Clarence Brown that year; he played James Stewart as a boy in *Of the Human Heart*. He was also scheduled after *Boys Town*, as the rising star at Metro, to play Spencer Tracy's son in a version of *The Yearling*. Directed by Clarence Thomas, this picture was shelved until after World War II ended. By then Gregory Peck and Claude Jarman, Jr., played the roles. Clarence Thomas remained director.

Tracy hated location work with its adverse conditions; Florida was not to his liking. He spent a few weeks out there with the mosquitos and heat and was happy to be off the prestigious *Yearling* production in two weeks. Gene had great respect for Tracy and Stewart, "great to work with. Tracy could focus. He had good technique. Very natural. Timeless. Even if the scripts or stories he acted in don't stand the test of time, his acting does hold up. Absolutely timeless." A few years later, Gene had the opportunity to do *Edison the Man* with Tracy, but the classic Marjorie Kinnan Rawlings story went to others.

Based on a report Gene heard many years later from a friend, and his own observations, stars like Tracy were highly protective of themselves. And, someone like Tracy with his devastating personal problems was inclined to maintain his privacy. Spencer would never ask a favor of Eddie Mannix or Howard Strickling, lest he jeopardize himself and be under their debt. "Tracy kept it all inside," concluded Reynolds. "He worked so hard and so much, and seems to have repressed so much. He sat on his anger, and it led him to become quite depressed in his older years."

The picture was rapidly proceeding with musical numbers performed by the Choir from Boys Town and the election hall scenes, filmed in an old gymnasium building on the Metro lot. The setting was also used for several assembly scenes and a boxing match between Freddie and Whitey.

One assembly sequence required Gene Reynolds, wearing a one-inch, elevated platform shoe, to trip and lose his balance. At this Mickey was supposed to make some insensitive remarks about the handicap, which led Tony (Gene) to run into Father Flanagan's arms in tears. "I was supposed to have a club foot," mentioned Gene. The shoe was quite uncomfortable and usually at lunch he would change his shoes to his own. Often, however, he simply forgot to bring his own shoes along so and had to endure the cramped leg.

Reynolds recalled that he "had four wardrobe changes. If I had been smarter back then, I would have tagged each costume and matched it with the Call Sheet so I didn't have to have that shoe on all day." Though Gene berated himself for this, he also said the fault rested with the studio system that caused everyone to feel insecure about his job. "Actually, the wardrobe man should have taught me. But, he was a volatile man, exasperated easily and very cranky. Like so many, he was worried that he must do a good job. His name was Red . . . and he was typical of production people. They were afraid."

Here too was a case of Jack Mintz and the influence he exerted on Taurog. When they first did the scene with Gene falling down, Mintz felt the director had an important message to create. A crippled boy struggling with a folding chair, Gene suggested to contemporary audiences the heroism of President Franklin Roosevelt who had himself overcome such adversity, as he suffered from polio. Taurog stressed the FDR parallel. To Gene it simply proved that Taurog "was simply not in the class of the great artistic directors like John Ford or Clarence Brown."

Crying scenes were the bane of Gene's career as a juvenile actor. When he fell into Tracy's arms, his eyes had to be moist. Once he did the master shot in a film with Jackie Cooper, crying exactly where they wanted. Then, to avoid the SAG (Screen Actors Guild) Meal Penalty, the crew broke. Gene was ready for his close-up and tears, but there was a long lunch break, then he played some ball. When they came back to film his close-up, "I was dry."

Jackie Cooper recommended camphor to be blown into his eyes, but Gene felt that was cheating. "I'm trying to cry, but nothing happens. Here's fifty people standing around waiting for this kid to cry." The stress put upon children in this situation was overwhelming, but it was their job and what they were hired to do.

The assistant director kept checking his watch and making Gene feel terrible. He told Jackie that his Uncle Norman insisted that good actors did not need those devices. Speaking the words, the tears came, pouring out. They had their shot.

Crying was an art for Bobs Watson. "Boy, could Bobs cry," said one of the cast. He was called upon many times in *Boys Town* for the waterworks to flow. In the studio scenes between them, Bobs found Spencer Tracy quiet and warm. Of all the juvenile performers, according to Bobs, he enjoyed closeness to Tracy, far more than anyone else. "Often after a scene, he'd reach over and hug me and take me on his lap. I felt like a little puppy. I would follow along and stand close, hoping he'd call me over, and often he would. He'd say: 'How are you doing?' and put his arm around me." It was behavior few others could recall, or would be willing to dispute. Henry Hull thought Tracy kept his distance from all the boys in the cast. Frankie Thomas concurred.

In his interview with Dickie Moore, Bobs revealed, "The crybaby of Hollywood, they called me. The reason they called me the crybaby of Hollywood was because my face got all screwed up. I don't know where all the crying came from, other than I had a very sensitive father that I loved very much, and he always explained to me what was happening in a scene. He'd say, 'How would you feel if this were your real father?' I can't explain it, but when tears were needed, I cried, and they were honest and real."

Whatever devotion to his father Bobs expressed, there was a counter view. Gene Reynolds overheard his mother talking to his father after a day at the studio "after a group of us had tested for a part. The test called for us to cry. She told Dad that Mr. Watson had said to Bobs, 'You cry now or you'll cry when you get home.'" When asked about this, Bobs vehemently denied it ever occurred. Moore reported: "He referred to his father as a loving relationship and how he enjoyed having him on the set, spending so much time with him. Bobs told me how much he still misses his Dad. And Bobs cried."

Actress Ann Rutherford was present during one incident near the set of a movie she made with Bobs. According to what she saw, Bobs was rambunctious on the set one day, and "his father called him aside and checked his watch. Then he whispered into the boy's ear, which horrified the child. He immediately went out and did the scene exactly." Coy Watson admitted to Rutherford that he told his son, "His dog would have to be sent to the pound unless he did this scene within the next ten minutes."

Bobs also told Dickie Moore that it was the eye contact of Tracy and Rooney that made their performances so compelling. "As they looked at you, they became the characters they were portraying . . . . They literally became those characters in very interesting way; they were performers at the controls, but they took on the personalities of the characters they were playing."

The pint-sized child star displayed cuteness that was a photocopy of Shirley Temple. Yet, he sincerely believed in the scenes he performed, giving his acting its own unique style. "In *Boys Town*, when Mickey Rooney left, it really broke my heart. It was a simple as that. I used to see Rooney and Spencer Tracy in a very idealized way."

Everyone carried Bobs around the set or in a movie. At least that was what Watson said to everyone he met from the old days. He quoted Mickey Rooney's plea to his mother, "'Hey, Mom, why can't you get me a little brother like this?' Bobs swore Mickey Rooney "used to rock me on the set when I was just a baby."

Eddie Norris portrayed Mickey Rooney's gangster brother who asked Father Flanagan to take care of the boy. Photo from the author's collection.

One of the pivotal action scenes of the film was done at Metro in the old gymnasium. The scene was a boxing match between Freddie and Whitey, with Father Flanagan officiating as the referee. Frankie Thomas and Mickey Rooney wore their silk trunks, and Spencer Tracy—remaining in costume as Flanagan—would oversee the fight. A ring was set up near the stage and extras were on hand as the emotionally charged spectator crowd.

Taurog chose one of the imported Omaha choirboys for a potential cameo; he wanted to wring tears from the toughest looking lad among them for a close-up.

Regarding this, Frankie Thomas said he watched Norman meet his Waterloo. "After we came back from Boys Town, we had this little kid who had this colorful history, and Taurog had him in front of the camera and was talking to him in an effort to make him cry. And that kid wasn't going to cry for anybody. I was surprised Taurog tried. He tried to mesmerize and cause this boy into crying—and it wouldn't happen. So we wound up with Bobs Watson who could cry at the drop of a hat."

Early in the picture, Mickey's character had challenged Freddie to a fight. Frankie revealed, "That whole scene is wrapped up in the line that I deliver, 'I will let you know when I am ready'. It said all you needed to know about the character."

There was no choreographing for the fight, claimed Thomas. No stunt expert was on the set, and apparently nobody thought it might be wise to have a medic nearby. Rooney had his vaudeville training and could take a pratfall, which the scene required.

Frankie Thomas insisted he had no need for an advisor or technical expert to train him. "I had been a welterweight on my school team. And my father was keen on boxing. My family owned a house about five miles from Madame Bay's Training Camp, where Joe Louis trained. We used to go up there to watch the fighters train." Describing an implausible situation, Frankie Thomas went on to say the intricate and dangerous moves of the filmed boxing match were "only rehearsed in generalities."

Keeping his back to the screen, Mickey did his best to break up Frankie by mugging. In the finished film, viewers can still glimpse Frankie fighting off a laugh as he threw a punch. Thomas gave the standard estimate: "Mickey probably would have been a pretty good fighter. He was light yet quite strong. He was very good in the ring." It almost sounded like a press release when he spoke the words.

Regarding the scene, Frankie had more to say about boxing with Rooney. "Now I had already had boxing lessons, but he took the punches. He made the fight look good. There was always the possibility that one of us could lose teeth. There were no mouth-guards. The actors never thought of these worries. The idea of getting hurt or protecting ourselves never occurred. It wasn't possible. When his back was to the camera was my cue for a left, and he was ready, pretending to be hit."

According to this account, Taurog apparently felt Rooney's extensive professional background relieved him of directorial involvement. Perhaps Jack Mintz didn't supply ideas about this sequence, though after one weak punch from Frankie, Rooney hilariously flew backward as if hit by Jack Dempsey. Frankie explained, "No, the director did not get in there and tell us to go this way and this way. When actors delivered what he wanted, Norman let them alone."

Pressed further on the boxing scene, Frankie also suggested that the few rounds "left Mick a bit winded." This explanation strained credibility as Rooney was a vivacious dancer and acrobat. "Well," noted Frankie. "He was living quite a life in those days. He was not in bed at 10pm every night."

Thomas explained some of the moves in the film. "We could always do the cross which was easy. They were looking at him—but didn't see me." The complicated set-up and shoot did not take long. "I guess it was after we did the long shots that we did the close-ups. I'd say the entire sequence took one afternoon."

After filming was done, Taurog sent Mickey and Frankie to the upper floor of the gymnasium, where awaited a *masseur*. "They gave Mickey about a forty-five minute rub to make him feel better—and then they gave me the same thing."

Shortly before he died, Henry Hull spoke about the making of *Boys Town*. In his recollections, he provided a strange story about Tracy and the boxing ring. "I don't remember Spence getting particularly close to any of the boys, including Rooney, but he put on the boxing gloves with one of the bigger kids one day, just fooling around, and one kid jabbed Spence's head off, and Spence got mad."

"Hull said Tracy put on gloves?" This account astounded Frankie Thomas, who retorted: "It could have happened, but I would say it did not. Hull doesn't have to make statements to the press. Hull would never make up a story like that. Tracy might have clowned around, but it seems unlikely. If he sparred with anyone famous like Mickey, it would have hit *Variety*. I don't think this report is correct." Frankie conceded, "After the fight they sent the two of us to be rubbed down, and it could have happened while we were upstairs. It's possible. I still don't think so . . ."

Young Frankie Thomas and veteran actor Henry Hull found themselves at a local watering hole one night after filming. Hull, with his long family history in the theater, also shared mutual friends with the young film actor and his family.

Frankie enjoyed one of his hobbies, sitting down with a veteran character actor to listen to the stories of the "Old Days." He always felt these mature actors were so good as storytellers because they re-enacted their memories and made one feel he was there with them in their adventures.

"I know I spent two lovely evenings in the company of Henry Hull. He was drinking scotch and water, and I was drinking ginger-ales, but we talked for hours."

Mr. Thomas believed he and Hull socialized at Boys Town, but according to the archives of Girls and Boys Town, Henry Hull was not present on the site, and no photographs of him at Boys Town in 1938 exist. After so many years have gone by, Frankie's recollections may be at fault about this. All of Hull's scenes with Tracy in Flanagan's Boys Town office or 'outdoors' were done on a stage or set at MGM.

Spencer Tracy socialized at Metro with few people in the cast except for Henry Hull, another Lambs member. Though Hull was known as a heavy imbiber, Tracy and Hull did not become drinking buddies on this picture, thanks to the watchful presence of Frank Whitbeck.

Most of the cast never saw the real Boys Town in Nebraska, and many from the first half of the movie, who worked at MGM in early July, 1938, never met or saw anyone who acted in the second half in late July of 1938. Martin Spellman never actually worked with Mickey Rooney. He never met Father Flanagan.

All of the scenes with Eddie Norris as Mickey's brother were second half storyline and filmed at Metro, but Lesley Fenton's death row scenes were done during the first two weeks of July at MGM. All scenes with Addison Richards were also studio-bound.

Frank Thomas knew most of the character actors well and had little interaction with them because the scenes were so segmented and shot on different days. If you weren't in a scene with an actor, chances were you did not see them on the set. "Addy Richards was only at the studio and never went to Boys Town with us. Minor Watson who played the bishop never visited at Boys Town or Omaha. Minor Watson was a good friend of mine. He was not a relationship to Bobs in a million years. He had appeared in *Angels Wash Their Faces*. He made a great hit in *State of the Union* on stage . . . stole it from Ralph Bellamy. Minor was a wonderful guy."

The picture was filled with faces that would appear again and again in movies and, later, television. John Hamilton was the prison warden in the opening scene, and later he was Perry White in the *Superman* TV series. George Humbert played Calatieri, the Italian shopkeeper, and continued in movies for twenty years, always, it seemed, cast as a headwaiter. Playing a member of Eddie Norris's gang, Jay Novello, with his twitchy little mustache, showed up weekly on television for a decade or two. As sheriff, Victor Killian became a familiar face, rising to his biggest popularity in old age on *Mary Hartman, Mary Hartman*.

There was no wrap party. Actors like Henry Hull, Ed Norris, and Leslie Fenton were off on other projects. Many of the cast were free-lancers and were then at other studios, some at Monogram or other Poverty Row pictures. The social parties that Sid Miller and Gene Reynolds had to attend, part of the business, were Metro affairs, arranged by the studio. If you weren't under an MGM contract, they had no interest in inviting actors to a serving of free publicity. The MGM players usually made hasty exits from these press affairs. Photo set-ups were just another bit of acting.

As the film neared the end of production, Frankie Thomas stood outside of the large hangar-like building where the scenes were done. "I was chatting with a girl outside the studio, trying to charm her. All of a sudden the door flies open and out comes a bunch of them, Mickey, Sidney Miller, Gene Reynolds, Bobs, and a few other boys in the cast, all in a row, like ducks. They walked around and around us."

After a couple of seconds, Mickey said, "You're not making any time, kid."

Shortly thereafter, the production was finished, but movie history still lay ahead.

10

POST-PRODUCTION

Fired from MGM before the filming began on his screenplay, Dore Schary sat at home all during the production. Having no means or income, he went through all his savings, sold one of his cars, and prepared to return to New York as a defeated man, with a pregnant wife due at any time. No one had remembered the screenwriter for months, and all during location shoots and studio work, Schary was totally ignored—until the editing process commenced.

The picture's first showing in September was a sneak preview at an Inglewood, California, theater. The day before the secret screening Considine called Schary and asked him to attend the screening at a movie house a few miles from the Culver City studio. At this point, Schary learned he would receive credit as screenwriter with Eleanor Griffin and story credit with John Meehan. For a man with a pregnant wife whose funds were running out, this was manna from heaven. Schary and his wife Miriam prepared for a last bit of fun before returning to the East.

When one of the major forces at the studio, being at the elbow of Mayer, Eddie Mannix mentioned to Considine that Schary ought to be at the preview, he heard for the first time an unpleasant story. Considine related Schary's dismissal months earlier by Harry Rapf. Furious at the injustice, Eddie Mannix scrambled to bring Dore Schary back on board the MGM team.

Considine made it clear to everyone how the studio had an important picture ready for accolades, and the race was on to release the movie before the holiday seasons. If *Boys Town* won awards and critical acclaim and the public learned the writer had been fired, Louis B. Mayer would be livid. When the buzz regarding *Boys Town* reached other studios, their competitive spirit might result in hiring Schary out from under MGM. Under those circumstances, Mannix paved the way for the immediate return of Dore to the studio. He offered Schary a raise in salary to $1,000 per week to return to his post.

The writer was present for the first major post-production meeting. Considine wanted to bring Schary in for meetings with Mayer, but Dore and L.B. had a destiny that meant their relationship would hinge on a future discussion. Mayer liked Schary and his ideas about movies and would promote him over the man who twice fired him.

Schary himself knew little about the production issues during June and July. Away from the studio with his wife and no job, he was without contact concerning the daily grind of filming his screenplay. He had no inkling of its progress or potential for success. An unemployed writer was unimportant in the industry, but one whose story was Oscar-bound might prove an embarrassment to MGM.

With thirty to fifty major films from each major studio annually, the demand for a solid script-writer remained a constant need. Schary understood MGM instinctively, recognizing that he had an obligation to reach all kinds of people with a tale's wide appeal.

In doing so, Schary later acknowledged: "a story must be 'for us.' It must fit our program, permit practical casting, and generally be ready to go . . . . It must be adaptable to visual telling, contain fresh pictorial elements to satisfy the audience eye, must be built around strong and intriguing characters (preferably with a good part for one of our contract stars), permit telling on the screen in not much more than ninety minutes, be non-topical enough not to date before we get our investment back."

Working with unusual haste, Elmo Veron finished his edits on September 1st, 1938, in time for the preview at Inglewood. Veron accomplished this feat because he was putting together segments as he received them. Considine gave his approval to this process. It could not have been possible during the Thalberg years.

While the crew continued to film at the studio over the past few weeks, Veron had been able to splice together all the prologue material, or slightly less than half the film's footage. His script with dialogue and continuity was dated the first day of September.

Considine was eager to test the film, which he believed could be ready sooner than nearly any other MGM picture, cashing in on the Rooney popularity and the recent Tracy Oscar for *Captains Courageous*.

During the screening, Schary listened with delight to the reactions to his version of the story: the audience loved every moment. Their emotions ran the gamut from laughter to tears. As the film ended, the audience was in ecstasy and pandemonium reigned in the lobby. Taurog and Considine were elated, and congratulations for this production with small expectations sweetened the pride of the Metro team.

During the din of accolades at Inglewood, Mannix was eager to hear what other pictures Schary worked on, and he told Schary he wanted to see him at his office in the morning. Word had trickled down that L.B. had a few reservations with the film.

Considine mobilized immediately. He and Taurog believed the film, already short, did not need to be cut down to ninety minutes. One scene mentioned as fodder for the cutting room was the boxing match between Rooney and Frankie Thomas.

One man sent word through Eddie Mannix that Mayer did not have a good feeling about the new picture—and his opinion counted more than anyone else at the studio. Louis B. Mayer believed the film would not attract an audience without a love story, but he was particularly bothered by the boxing match between Freddy Fuller (Frank Thomas) and Whitey Marsh (Mickey Rooney), deemed too violent for the image of Andy Hardy and the reputation of the studio.

Part of Mayer's usual reservation centered on violence in any storyline, which he felt out of place in the escapist world of his motion pictures. His stronger sense was that Andy Hardy ought not to behave in this fashion. Image dominated the studio's star system. Mayer wanted to cut the three-minute boxing sequence, the culmination of the long simmering rivalry between two characters.

Considine and Taurog knew this would delay the picture's release and damage the effect of the message. It also happened to be a highly entertaining moment that especially appealed to boys in the audience. It may also be that Rooney by himself went to Mayer to defend his performance in the pratfall-laden boxing scene. Rooney was not inclined to play Andy Hardy off-screen and may have believed he must demonstrate his need to spread his acting wings on-screen.

Mickey claimed to have given Mayer a piece of his mind on this issue, but the story came sixty years later. "Well," Rooney explained: "I just remember Mr. Tracy and myself, we went in and I said to Mr. Mayer, "Mr. Mayer, you've got to release *Boys Town*."

Whether Tracy felt strongly enough to go to Mayer is not confirmed by any other source. The boxing contest was not his fight, literally or figuratively. Spencer Tracy noted in his personal journal on that Friday before Labor Day, he was off playing polo at his favorite country club, and he played sets all day. Though Mickey Rooney contended years later that he and Tracy went into L.B.'s office in a snit to support their film, it seems unlikely.

According to Mickey, L.B. responded by initially complaining: "But it's got no sex in it, Mickey. There are no songs." However doubtful it may be that Mayer would be so short-sighted, Mickey insisted he made a grand pitch to the big man: "It's a song of freedom. It's a song of rehabilitation. It's the song of youth no matter what color or faith you are. It's about praying. It's about living a good life."

Rooney conceded Mayer's answer. "He said, 'Okay.' We didn't give him any place else to go." If the head of the studio had true reluctance to use the scene in question, it would have ended up lost in some film canister. Mayer also had a reputation of putting forth an argument to see how strongly people believed in their case. He may have been testing Taurog, Considine, and Rooney, to see the level of their commitment to the integrity of the scene.

The MGM agenda next involved Father Flanagan in a special screening at the studio. Once again haste seemed to mark this approach; within two days a luncheon for a few dignitaries with L.B. and several hundred of the key studio people was arranged. Howard Strickling was in charge of publicity, and he arranged for a flag-draped hall, catered with the superior food from the MGM commissary.

Msg. Flanagan and his bishop arrived by rail from Omaha for the big event. Strickling lost no opportunities to plant items with the press. A short documentary on Boys Town could also use clips of the banquet. Besides a cadre of Catholic film stars, Mayer made certain that Will Hays, a politician of the Warren G. Harding era who set up a censorship board on motion pictures in lieu of federal intervention, was present at this wholesome depiction of a priest's efforts on behalf of wayward youth.

Harold Heffernan, a well-known Hollywood columnist of the era, quoted Mr. Mayer as telling Father Flanagan before the studio banquet, "Just as soon as I can find a priest who can match your broad vision and general understanding of the youth, I will dedicate the remainder of my life and money to the establishment of such a community as Boys Town right here in Los Angeles."

Bishop James Ryan was also a guest at the luncheon for Father Flanagan, as were Los Angeles clergymen of all denominations, and such movie celebrities as Don Ameche, Jackie Cooper, George Murphy, Maureen O'Sullivan, and Dennis O'Keefe. The list of guests among the film actors included most notable Roman Catholics. At the testimonial, only film clips of key scenes were shown to the audience, in order to whet their appetite for the premieres in New York City and in Omaha. During the banquet, Father Flanagan requested the film first be shown in Omaha.

Louis B. Mayer held a luncheon for Father Flanagan on September 1ˢᵗ, 1938, to honor the priest for his work and to preview movie clips for many studio executives, the stars, and friends of the cleric. Photo from the author's collection.

The condensed preview was acclaimed as a 'tremendous success and the audience broke into applause at several points" according to a dispatch from Hollywood. "The fiction is deeply moving and left an apparent indelible impression upon the minds of an audience which included, besides regular citizens of Westwood representative from the biggest newspaper syndicates."

After the lunch, a series of photo opportunities showed the guests with the honored priest. Newsreel footage was made of Tracy and Flanagan together. On that occasion, having seen the film, and somewhat non-plussed, Father Flanagan offered the comment: "I'd hate to have to play Spencer Tracy in a motion picture."

After acceding to Father Flanagan's wishes for a premiere in his home parish, a rush of work needed to be done. On the first of September, 1938, in Nebraska, parallel celebrations were underway. Local dignitaries and politicians oversaw "efforts to make the show a memorable civic event were under way on several fronts." As a gesture to the character building occurring at Boys Town, Mayor Butler and the Omaha City Council offered to become ordinary citizens on September 7th, and the mayor of Boys Town and his commissioners would assume the duties of their official counterparts for several hours. By Butler's proclamation September 7th was called Boys Town Day.

Boys Town commissioners were Robert Paradise, police; Johnny Waskiewicz, public works; Sam Turner, public welfare; Tom McGuire, health, and Clinton Simmons, fire and safety, and Jesse Ruiz, parks. Accompanying Mayor Jack Farrald, they visited Mayor Butler at City Hall to arrange take over the city administration. As did Mayor Butler, Mayor Farrald issued a proclamation naming the showing of the new movie as "Premiere Day."

"Whereas a signal honor has been conferred upon our sister city," stated the proclamation, "and whereas the people and officials of Omaha, The Mutual Broadcasting system and the *World Herald* are ably and cordially assisting in making this premiere noteworthy, therefore be it enacted that Wednesday, September 7th, be designated as Premiere Day and that the citizens of Boys Town offer prayers of thanksgiving."

Catholic clergy throughout the Omaha diocese gave notice of the special day from their pulpits. Protestants ministers and Jewish leaders also pledged cooperation. After all, Boys Town was an ecumenical operation, respecting all faiths. The Chamber of Commerce, most service clubs, and many businessmen, also pledged their support, which expected to bring thousands of persons to Omaha from across the Midwest.

The local consortium of theatre owners made arrangements to care for the expected preview crowds inside and outside the Omaha theatre. A great number of mail orders began to arrive as soon as word went out, although the office did not open until Saturday. All seats were expected to be gone within two days, but actually were snapped up sooner. One problem emerged immediately with locals feeling chagrin that the film opening was "strictly formal." The publicity director issued a sudden explanation to allay the scores of complainers.

Fewer than 50 seats remained available at the Omaha theatre for the picture's premiere on Wednesday night. Manager of Omaha Theatre, Eddie Forrester, said about 600 of the two thousand seats were bought by out of town persons through mail orders. Among them was a $10 order from Spencer Tracy. All seats reserved a top price of $2, a hefty amount in the Depression Era of America.

Omaha's man in charge of publicity, Ted Emerson, allayed the worry of the many local citizens who bought seats for the movie show: "The formal dress announcement applied only to the Hollywood people and other distinguished guests. We don't care what people wear; they can come in evening clothes, in overalls, sarongs, bathing suits or Eskimo costumes. It doesn't matter."

The city organized a reception of Hollywood celebrities, including Spencer Tracy, Mickey Rooney, and Maureen O'Sullivan (who had no connection whatsoever to the film and came along for the ride) at Union Station when they arrived Tuesday evening. W.M. Jeffries, president of the Union Pacific, ordered the station suitably decorated for the occasion. The Union Pacific announced posters urging out of state people to attend the premiere had been placed in every station in the Omaha transit system

Plans for the gala came from forty high-minded Omaha civic leaders at the Chamber of Commerce. This powerful group of Omahans included Msgr. James W. Stenson, Rev. A.K. Stewart head of the Ministerial union, Rev. Charles Durdin of First Baptist Church, Rabbi Frederick Cohn, Henry Monsky (whose character was played by the pseudonymous Henry Hull), and Rev. Louis Demars (Monsignor Flanagan's close associate at Boys Town).

Pressure was on the community, according to Francis P Matthews who said: "The eyes of the nation will be on Omaha Wednesday evening. If we carry off the premiere of this movie satisfactorily, it will be a great triumph for Omaha." This was echoed by Eddie Forrest who added "in recognition of his years of effort at his boys home, Father Flanagan will see Omaha repay him with this tribute."

Emerson also outlined plans for bleachers, with which Mayor Butler took issue, noting they would not hold the crowds. The Mayor was correct. Emerson also told the Chamber of Commerce to employ customary Hollywood elegance, with searchlights, spotlights, carpeted sidewalks and other touches. All the ideas were enthusiastically endorsed. They had little time to implement all the recommendations.

Governors of six states and other distinguished visitors received invitations to attend the premiere and to be guests of Bishop Ryan at a reception at his home.

Twenty blocks in the downtown district were decorated with American flags. Centerpieces hanging form trolley wires bore the legend, 'Welcome Father Flanagan' and 'Home of Boys Town.' The city's decorations extended roughly from the area between Fiftieth and Seventeenth streets from Harney to Dodge. All costs were covered by a fund-raising effort by the city's Chamber of Commerce.

Twice the seven thousand persons who greeted Spencer Tracy and Mickey Rooney in June were on hand for the ceremonies at Union Station. Father Flanagan and the Hollywood party left Culver City after the banquet and arrived in Omaha by exactly on time Tuesday evening. They were aboard the Los Angeles Limited. Besides the film's stars, Maureen O'Sullivan, Father Flanagan, Bishop Ryan, Director Norman Taurog, Producer John Considine and Mrs. Considine, enjoyed the festivities. Also along was Frank Whitbeck, described as advertising director, keeping company with Spencer Tracy.

At Union Station Mayor Jack Farrald of Boys Town extended greetings on behalf of 212 boys at the village home. Omaha's Mayor Butler presented the stars with a floral key, and also presented his welcome in the form of a floral heart. Nebraska's Governor Cochran welcomed the visitors on behalf of the state.

Word sent from the Los Angeles convent of the Sacred Heart revealed that Maureen O'Sullivan was a graduate of a Sacred Heart school in Dublin, which led to an addition to the welcoming ceremony at union station tonight. On behalf of the alumni and students of Duchesne College, a Sacred Heart institution, Mary Claire Matthews presented Miss O'Sullivan with a bouquet of flowers. Elizabeth Ann Davis, queen of Ak Sar Ben, made a similar presentation to Mrs. John Considine, wife of the producer.

A detail of 110 police and 40 firemen served as crowd control during the boisterous premiere. Robert Munch, Assistant Chief of Police and Jonas Francis, Assistant Fire Chief coordinated elaborate plans for blocking off Douglas Street and for handling upwards of 25,000 spectators.

The cavalcade of stars, celebrities, and guests, motored with police escort to the Omaha Theatre through the throng of cheering citizens. Hugh Cutler, manager of the Shrine Band of Tangier Temple, led his organization of seventy musicians, dressed in their colorful costumes, and they played in front of the Omaha Theatre from 7:30 to 7:45 on that night.

Outside the Omaha Theatre the movie celebrities and Father Flanagan were introduced to speak over public address and regional radio hookups. The premiere was broadcast over 107 stations and radio outlets.

The Mutual Broadcasting System carried the ceremonies on live radio, Wednesday night from 7:45 to 8:30 pm according to James Douglass, program director for the Central States Broadcasting System. Local radio outlet KOIL originated the program broadcast.

Part of the production was the inclusion of a performance of the Boys Town Choir, singing two numbers during the ceremonies. Unseen by the radio audience, special scenery created for their road show came from Chicago to serve as background for the choir. One of their selections was a newly arranged piece, entitled "Boys Town," a tune written especially for their national tour, commencing within the next few weeks. The choir's publicity only added to the growing success of the motion picture.

After the opening of the picture, MGM gave Father Flanagan an embossed scrapbook of the special premiere in Omaha.

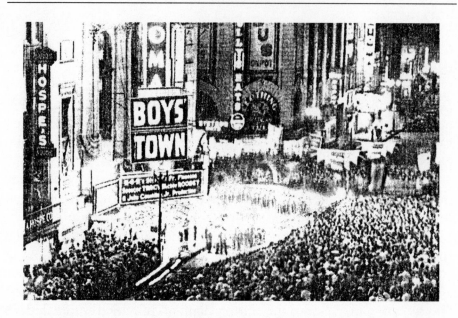

The Omaha Theatre in the state's capitol city hosted a major Hollywood-style premiere for Boys Town, complete with searc lights, formal dress for the stars, and red carpets. Photo courtesy of the Omaha World Tribune.

Culminating in three Oscars, the picture thrust Spencer Tracy into Hollywood legend, winning his second Oscar in two years. It also made Dore Schary one of the most important people in motion pictures. He immediately began a script of *Edison the Man* for Tracy. Within a few years he would be in charge of MGM's high quality B-movie list, and he would replace L.B. Mayer himself a decade later.

Ironically, for Boys Town and Father Flanagan, the film brought them to the brink of disaster. Because the picture showed a highly successful operation, growing constantly with good clothes and good facilities, donations to Boys Town dropped to nothing.

The shocking result of popular success for the studio and the performers left Father Flanagan mulling the reasons he did not benefit more from the motion picture. In an interview later, the priest admitted he was not quite sure why it happened. In analyzing the situation Flanagan considered most people, seeing the picture, rather took it for granted that an orphanage sufficiently famed to be the subject of a movie, was a thoroughly established institution. The MGM picture presented Father Flanagan as a financial wizard who could always pick a few hundred thousand out of the air. While the founder of Boys Town had, in fact, been a fund-raiser with *panache*, the movie brought this to a halt.

The film created a tidal wave of boys who wanted to enter Boys Town, and the wave came directly to the door of Father Flanagan. No longer did the waifs trickle into Omaha one at a time, but a flood of boys requested assistance. The priest speculated that the number showing up at his village doubled after the movie's initial release. It was not unusual to have ten boys show up in a day. Lacking resources, he could not make a permanent home for the majority of them. Only the most needy cases were allowed to stay.

One Omaha friend of Father Flanagan, possibly Henry Monsky, wrote L.B. Mayer, suggesting that, in view of the picture's success, the five thousand dollar fee might be hoisted a bit. Mayer replied that he'd have to take it up with the corporation and that he'd be glad to make a personal donation.

Msgr. Flanagan definitely did not believe MGM owed him anything. Though the movie told of plans for new buildings, everything he wanted was on hold. Two years later, it was reported Flanagan took out the plans every few days to go over them lovingly. They called for a building program estimated around $1.5M. The plans included four apartments, each to hold 130 boys with compact dormitory unit under a proctor; a dining room and kitchen, and chapel. Adding these buildings, the capacity of the home for boys, would be nearly tripled.

New friends like Spencer Tracy and Mickey Rooney constantly lent their names and influence to fund-raising letters and other means to increase the revenue. Tracy wrote a letter to patrons of Boys Town, telling them that the Home did not receive any residuals or proceeds from the film. What it finally came down to was another film, a sequel needed to stress how much money Boys Town required and was not able to raise. This did not appeal to the priest. Father Flanagan took to telling anyone who'd listen that another movie might cause him to fall short in making operating expenses.

In 1939 and 1940 receipts ran about $5000 less than for previous year. And, though the home had no debt, it also had no money, except for about $50,000 in a trust fund from which only the income could be used. What truly brought Father Flanagan to the idea that a sequel movie was needed was his desire to make "Americans realize the brutal conditions which existed in reform schools." According to Boys Town historian, Tom Lynch, the priest worked his entire life to close every reform school in America.

"Father was asked by the Governor of California to help reform the Whittier Reform School, where boys were committing suicide due to the brutality of the guards," stated Lynch. "The film *Men of Boys Town* contains scenes of brutality based upon the documented reports of abuse in the Whittier Reform School. Both movies were a part of Father Flanagan's mission to change the way children were treated in America, and around the world."

One boy who watched the filming and lived in the area for the rest of his life, Hank Avilla, said in later years: "I thought the movie would go on, but not to this magnitude. I was amazed at the longevity. I tell you what, the good that Boys Town has consistently given— and I think indirectly the movie—had a great influence on this place because prior to that time we had difficulty getting something to eat and maintaining this place and then all of a sudden people started finding out, "Well, gee, there is a Boys Town and they're doing some good and as a result people started sending in a dollar here and a dollar there and that certainly continued on. Now you have a beautiful place that we have here for the kids and to carry on Father Flanagan's dream."

Though Tracy won the Oscar and received glowing reviews, most of the attention from critics and moviegoers centered on Mickey Rooney's flamboyant work. Instead of a supporting Oscar, Mickey received a miniature honorary statue for "bringing to the screen the spirit and personification of youth, and as a juvenile player setting a high standard of ability and achievement."

Despite his misgivings at first about playing a priest again, Tracy would do it a third time in 1961 for *The Devil at Four O'Clock*, and turned down many other offers to play clerics during the following decades of his career. He believed enough in the role of Father Flanagan to reprise it in the sequel. At the Academy Award Motion Picture ceremony in 1939, he humbly responded: "I won't feel that I can accept this as a tribute to my performance, but I do accept it as a tribute to the man who inspired the picture."

Robert Wagner, film star and protégé to Tracy, and a man who knew the star better than most, believed Spencer Tracy genuinely and truly appreciated the opportunity to play Flanagan. "Spencer Tracy created a natural style of acting. . . . As Father Flanagan, you take what he did in that. It was that energy going on inside of him. He made that material come alive."

The day after Spencer Tracy won the Best Actor Oscar for his performance in this film, an MGM publicist released a statement—without consulting Tracy first—that the actor would donate his Oscar to the real *Boys Town* in Nebraska. In a recent interview Robert Wagner insisted that the idea was likely Spencer's out of his admiration for Father Flanagan.

Tracy made the donation and expected the Academy of Motion Pictures would send him a replacement Oscar. When the replacement arrived, the engraving on the award read: "Best Actor—Dick Tracy." Tracy's original award remained on Father Flanagan's desk for the next ten years, given to the man he credited for his performance.

Boys endlessly came into his office and started a tradition of rubbing the Oscar for good luck. Previously, they would rub the fur of Carlo the dog, the stray mutt that was the unofficial mascot of the Town, stuffed by a taxidermist until the creature mysteriously disappeared around the time the Oscar showed up. Tracy's gold statuette is on display in the Village of Boys Town Hall of History.

Mickey Rooney reported: "*Boys Town* was big box office, my biggest . . . The movie also put the real Boys Town on everyone's map and helped Father Flanagan raise millions in contributions. *Boys Town* not only made friends for Father Flanagan and money for Mr. Mayer. It won an Oscar for Spencer Tracy. That year I won an Oscar too . . . 'For personification of youth.' Whatever that meant."

Rooney's final encounter with the new head of MGM, Dore Schary, ended unpleasantly ten years after their shared movie. Suffering sagging box-office because of the hoary Andy Hardy series, the post-war years lessened Mickey's appeal to youth. "I expected Schary to retain some fond memories of our successes together, but from him I got zilch. Maybe it was because of the scene we'd had when I returned from the army. I went up to his office as soon as I got home, still in uniform. 'Hi, kid,' said Schary. 'Where you been?' I couldn't believe his snotty words. How had he fought the war? I stared at him. I was still five feet three, but I had grown a little bit and I'd seen men die, and I thought I'd learned the difference between reality and fantasy. I spoke the last words I would ever speak to this man. I said, 'Fuck you, Schary.' Then I walked out of the room."

Director Norman Taurog won his Oscar for *Skippy* in 1931, but never achieved success like that again, not for *Boys Town*, nor its sequel. Nowadays he is among the forgotten directors of the past, cited for his pedestrian, studio-style. In his later years he directed Jerry Lewis and Dean Martin in several of their films. He then became Elvis Presley's favorite director and did nine pictures with the King.

Gene Reynolds continued acting, often in Andy Hardy movies at MGM. He left the acting part of the business and moved to New York in 1950, but went back into the fray as a director. His friend, Jackie Cooper, then producing his own series gave Gene work.

This led to success, directing a hit television series, *My Three Sons*, that starred Tim Considine, son of John who produced *Boys Town*. Gene continued to see all the boys for lunch regularly in the past forty years. Reynolds also went on too to produce *M*A*S*H** and *Lou Grant* on television, winning many accolades. Bob Considine, newspaper columnist and brother of John, wrote a short history of Boys Town for its fortieth anniversary in 1957, maintaining the ties to the institution.

Of his work in *Boys Town*, Reynolds noted: "The movie itself was a little sweet by today's standards, many were hokey in those days. The rescue scene was the weakest part of film at end, all done at Metro."

In the end Frankie Thomas remained bitter about his billing and his treatment by MGM. Instead of reaching the top studio and finding a home, he was cast back into the Universal world for a short movie career thereafter. The rejection and failure to be part of the sequel further wore down Frankie's goodwill about the motion picture industry. Though available, he was not cast in the sequel.

Martin Spellman's career lasted a few extra years. He starred in several films, but by the time the Second World War began, his boyish looks turned into gangly adolescent. He saw the bane of his movie stardom: "The problem comes when child stars are no longer 'cute' and are dumped, and they go out in the 'real' world for a job, and they cannot adjust." He stayed out of the movie business, raising a family and occasionally having his children (and grandchildren) see one of his old films on television.

And of Spencer Tracy's own thoughts about the *Boys Town* film, perhaps Frank McHugh heard it best when they were having drinks at the Lambs' Club in 1954, a famous actors group, in New York. "My father always wanted me to be a priest, but I disappointed him," was how McHugh related it, revealing Tracy's conversation. "Then, at the end, he said he was proud that I was a good actor, but he never lived long enough to see me in anything decent." McHugh revealed that, somewhat drunken, Tracy was on the verge of tears, lamenting, "Maybe I got the guilt. Maybe that's why I do my best when I play priests in my pictures, like Father Mullin in *San Francisco* and Father Flanagan in *Boys Town.*"

Louis B. Mayer, Edward J. Flanagan, and Spencer Tracy shared the podium during a luncheon at MGM only once, yet they remain tied together forever as a result of the movie biography about the founder of Boys Town. Photo from the author's collection.

The deposed head of MGM died in 1958; there was only one person to deliver his eulogy: Spencer Tracy. Much of what Tracy said about the impresario of Hollywood applied to Father Flanagan. "Louis B. Mayer knew people better than all the many things he knew so well. It was because he knew people that he was able to know the other many things. Such knowledge of people is a rare privilege. The story he wanted to tell was the story of America—the land for which he had an almost furious love, born of gratitude."

When Tracy died ten years later, the honor of speaking his eulogy went to Robert Wagner. In autumn of 2003, the Girls and Boys Town held their annual convention for alumni. Among the honored guests that year was Mickey Rooney. It had been sixty-six years since the filming on the campus. July 26 was the anniversary of the end of filming.

Gathering at the old gymnasium at the Wegner School, three hundred alums voted by acclamation to give Rooney this honor. "This is an honor to not be taken lightly and believe me I don't take it lightly," said Rooney. "I love Girls and Boys Town. I've made 350 pictures in my life, more than anyone in Hollywood. But the one that I treasure most is Boys Town."

After that came the unveiling of a plaque to designate Mickey as the Honorary Mayor for the rest of his life. The plaque's inscription said in part, "In the 65th anniversary year of the premier of the movie, Boys Town and in recognition of its worldwide impact, the citizens and alumni of Boys Town bestow upon our good friend, Mr. Mickey Rooney, the title of Honorary Mayor for Life."

The plaque found its place on the outside wall of the old gymnasium, one of the original facades used in the 1938 movie.

Spencer Tracy's family was invited to Girls and Boys Town in 2003 for the 65th anniversary of the motion picture. The latest generation of the Village lined up on a red carpet, extending fifty feet, to greet the family of the late star. This gave Tracy's family the first chance to hold the illustrious Oscar that he donated the day after it was won. A tile on the newly created Wall of Fame was dedicated to Tracy. His son, John, and grandson, Joe, attended with two of the actor's great-grandsons.

Dr. Patrick Brookhouser, Director of the Boys Town National Research Hospital, spoke during the ceremony of the liaison and partnership they held with the John Tracy Clinic, founded by Spencer and his wife Louise, which places its focus on deaf education and was named in honor of their son.

For over sixty-five years, and for the foreseeable future, Spencer Tracy and Father Flanagan will be forever linked together in their humanitarian efforts.

All of the events came about because of this inspirational movie, beloved by generations, made in black and white during the heyday of Metro-Goldwin-Mayer, receiving the Monsignor's heartfelt blessing.

Ten years after the movie's premiere, during a goodwill trip to war-ravaged Europe and its displaced children, Father Flanagan died in the midst of his intensive workload. As a fellow priest gave him final rites, he brushed his bushy eyebrows, breathed "Amen," and closed his eyes, leaving the earth a better place than he had found it . . .

ACKNOWLEDGEMENTS

Thanks must be given to the original "boys" of the film who consented to interviews decades later. Gene Reynolds provided his insights into the trip to Boys Town and the aftermath of decades. Martin Spellman left movies after a short career and gave his extraordinary memories of those days. Frankie Thomas went on to a career in television after playing in *Boys Town* gave us hours of interview time. Robert Wagner, the protégé of Spencer Tracy and major motion picture producer and actor, graciously provided his own perspective of Mr. Tracy, star of the film, and provided us with insights and advice on the true story. Our best wishes also go to Mickey Rooney, still the most active of all the performers of the movie, who visited Boston with his autobiographical one-man show during the writing of the book.

Research of the production came largely by the great library of the American Motion Picture Academy of Arts and Sciences. Archivist Barbara Hall provided assistance at the Margaret Herrick Library where Oscar lives year-round. Insights into the location work at Boys Town came too from Thomas J. Lynch, the historian in residence at Girls and Boys Town's Hall of History who could answer all the esoteric questions.

Additional information came from the archives of the Omaha Public Library and the *Omaha World Herald*.

Marvin Paige of Hollywood and New York whose career as a casting director makes him a font of knowledge gave his insights and expertise. Friends and faculty at Curry College once again provided a backbone of support: research funding came from Curry College's faculty support committee, and colleagues again lent their uplifting insights, especially Professor Nicholas J. Krach and Dr. Gabrielle Regney among others.

Without Barbara Merlin, who has the ability to transcend the most difficult Hollywood moments, we could not have written this book. She gave us yeoman assistance. Research Assistants on the East Coast were Priscilla Pope and Joshua Janson who provided their usual trouble-shooting skills.

BIBLIOGRAPHY

_____"An Alumni Movie Review," (Boys Town) *Alumni News*. Fall 2003, Vol. 42, Issue 3.

_____"Original Edition, replica of First News Letter," (Boys Town) *Alumni News*. Spring 2005, Vol. 44, Issue 1.

_____"Boys Town Choir to Sing at Premiere," *Omaha World Herald*. September 6, 1938.

_____"Boys Town Council Will Rule Omaha," *Omaha World Herald*, September 2, 1938.

_____"Boys Town Film Assured," *Omaha World Herald*, July 24, 1938.

Churchill, Douglas W. "Life of a Child Star," *New York Times*, May 22, 1938.

Churchill, Douglas W. "Metro Spends a Dollar Wisely," New York Times. July 31, 1938.

Considine, Bob. *Father Flanagan's Boys' Home*. Boys Town Press.

Cooper, Jackie with Dick Kleiner. *Please Don't Shoot My Dog*. William Morrow, 1981.

_____"Crowds to Greet Film Unit," *Omaha World Herald*, September 7, 1938.

Davidson, Bill *Spencer Tracy: Tragic Idol*. E.P. Dutton, 1987.

Eyman, Scott. *Lion of Hollywood: The Life and Legend of Louis B. Mayer*. Simon and Schuster, 2005.

_____"Flags to Fly for Premiere," *Omaha World Herald*, September 3, 1938.

Fleming, E.J. *The Fixers: Eddie Mannix, Howard Strickling, and the MGM Publicity Machine*. McFarland, 2005.

Gabler, Neal. *An Empire of Their Own: How the Jews Invented Hollywood*. Doubleday,1988.

_____"Heat Melts Discs," *Omaha World Herald*, July 4, 1938.

Kashner, Sam and Jennifer MacNair. *The Bad and the Beautiful*. W.W. Norton, 2002.

King, Alison. *Spencer Tracy*.

Lonnborg, Barbara. *Boys Town: a Photographic History*. Boys Town Press, 1992.

Lonnborg, Barbara and Thomas J. Lynch (eds.). *Father Flanagan's Legacy: Hope and Healing for Children*. Boys Town Press, 2003.

Lynch, Thomas J. *Interviews*. Summer, 2005.

Marx, Arthur. *The Nine Lives of Mickey Rooney*. Stein and Day, 1986.

McGilligan, Patrick. *George Cukor: a Double Life*. St. Martin's Press, 1991.

_____"Mickey Rooney Honored . . ." (Boys Town) *Alumni News*. Fall 2003, Vol. 42, Issue 3.

_____"Mickey Rooney to Receive Lifetime Membership . . ." (Boys Town) *Alumni News*. Summer, 2003, Vol.42, Issue 2.

_____"Mickey Rooney, the Glamorous," *New York Times*. July 24, 1938.

Montgomery, Elizabeth. *The Best of MGM*.

_____"Moppets on the March," *New York Times*. June 28, 1938.

Morrow, Edward. "Boys Town Movie Has Surprise Ending," *Omaha World Herald*, Oct. 23, 1938.

Moore, Dick. *Twinkle, Twinkle, Little Star*. Harper and Row, 1984.

_____"News of the Screen," *New York Times*, May 14, 1938.

_____"Norman Taurog Gets Five-Year Contract with Metro," *New York Times*. May 16, 1938.

Nugent, Frank S. "Screen in Review," *New York Times*. Sept. 9, 1938, p. 25.

Oursler, Fulton and Will. *Father Flanagan of Boys Town*. Doubleday, 1949.

Packer, Eleanor. *Mickey Rooney Himself*. Whitman Publishing, 1939.

Rooney, Mickey. *I.E., an Autobiography*. G.P.Putnam, 1965.

Reynolds, Gene. *Interview*. Summer, 2005.

Rooney, Mickey. *Life is Too Short*. Random House,1991.

Schary, Dore. *Case History of a Movie*. Random House, 1950.

Schary, Dore. *Heyday*. Berkley Books, 1970.

_____"Screen News Here and in Hollywood," New York Times. September 8, 1938.

_____"Stars Coming for Boys Town," *Omaha World Herald*, September 1, 1938.

Spellman, Martin. *Interviews*. Summer, 2005.

Swindell, Larry. *Spencer Tracy*. Signet, 1969.

Thomas, Bob. *Thalberg: Life and Legend*. New Millenium Press, 2000.

Thomas, Frankie. *Interviews*. Summer, 2005.

_____"Three Film Officials Here," *Omaha World Herald*, June 29, 1937.

_____"Tracy Gives Badges," *Omaha World Herald*, July 4, 1938.

Wagner, Robert. *Interviews*. Summer, 2005.

Wilson, Keith. "Boys Town Awaits Hollywood Troupe," *Omaha World Herald*, August 8, 1937.